Why
Are You Sitting
On Your
Greatness?

NORA SHARIFF-BORDEN

Danic Enjoy!

Greatness Awaits you

Love Nora Shariff :)

Printed in the United States of America

First Printing, 2019

Why Are You Sitting On Your Greatness?

WHY ARE YOU SITTING ON YOUR GREATNESS?

TABLE OF CONTENTS

Foreword	7
Preface	11
Special Thanks	12
Chapter 1	15
Chapter 2	33
Chapter 3	37
Chapter 4	53
Chapter 5	61
Chapter 6	81
Chapter 7	87
Chapter 8	93
Chapter 9	99
Chapter 10	107
Chapter 11	115
Chapter 12	121
Chapter 13	129
Chapter 14	149
Chapter 15	155
Chapter 16	215
Chapter 17	221

WHY ARE YOU SITTING ON YOUR GREATNESS?

FOREWORD

My mother has always seen in me what I have yet to discover within myself and I'm so thankful for this because it has caused her to continuously motivate me when I was unable to motivate myself! I've gone through life's struggles just like everyone else but the difference between me and many others is that I have a mom that refuses to just let me sit in my misery and give up! She has always shown me an alternate route to travel to find my way back home, to love, happiness and peace. Working with my mom all these years showed me the kind of woman that I aspire to become - someone who is always trying to use their gifts to bless others! I really enjoyed working with her on this most recent project, *Why Are You Sitting On Your Greatness* because it has allowed me to witness so many testimonies of all the women who I love and witnessed their success. To see where they came from and where they are now just gives me more of a push to keep on walking in my own greatness knowing that it will most definitely pay off!

Aishah Hassan

WHY ARE YOU SITTING ON YOUR GREATNESS?

FOREWORD

Greatness is a powerful tool and something that we all strive for daily. The word carries such a positive pattern for our lives – one in which we often think we cannot reach. On our own, we will never achieve the greatness we strive for, but walking hand-in-hand with God, we are able to achieve everything He has planned for our lives.

Nora's collection of empowering affirmations, quotes and stories truly shows us how to get up off of our greatness and step into the powerful and wonderful life God has chosen for us. These daily readings are life-changing. The personal stories and insights are relatable and encouraging. They show us that everyone walks through times of sitting on their greatness and how to overcome.

I have had the honor to work alongside Nora on her projects for the past several years. The friendship is one that inspires me and I thank God for allowing our paths to cross. Nora is authentic and truly enjoys seeing other women succeed. Why Are You Sitting on Your Greatness captures her passion and her own greatness. These writings will encourage and empower; they will make you smile and bring tears to your eyes.

Nora, thank you for listening to God's call and obediently sharing your heart. We are all better for it.

Stephanie Hunt
Owner
The Savvy Peach, LLC

WHY ARE YOU SITTING ON YOUR GREATNESS?

PREFACE

I believe reading this book will help you to understand why you are sitting on your greatness! Know this, you are on the brink of something Great! The enemy wants you to think you can't do it, that this is not for you, and that you don't have what it takes to be great, but God says that you have the power to be great! In 1st John 4:4 He tells us that greater is He that is in you than he that is in the world! God is telling us that we have the power and that the greater one is inside of us! The key is, you must listen to the voice of God and not the lies of the enemy! Ask yourself this question, what is stopping you from stepping into your greatness? I love what Pastor Andre' Gorham says in his book, "FEAR NOT", Whenever God wanted to do a great thing through His people, He always told them; "Fear Not!", whenever He wanted to manifest a mighty miracle with them, for them, and through them, He said, "Fear Not!"

Greatness awaits you; it is up to you to step into it!

Decide today that you will not sit on your greatness!

WHY ARE YOU SITTING ON YOUR GREATNESS?

SPECIAL THANKS

A special thanks to my Lord and Savior, Jesus Christ for believing in me when I did not believe in myself. I thank you for encouraging and breathing Your greatness into me. Thank you for showing me that I could write a book even when I thought I could not. Lord, You have breathed Your words into me and said, "write." Lord, I love you!

To my best friend and my husband, Neil. Thank you for your support and unconditional love. You have allowed me to be myself and I thank you for 40 years of love and friendship. I thank God for our togetherness in Christ. You are most definitely my soul mate. I love you.

To my mother, Audrey Jones, who showed me how to be the great woman and mother that I am today. Even when all the odds tried to prevent you from making it, you persevered and made it anyways. For that I thank you.

To my father, Clyde Morgan, thank you for your gifts and your many talents! I love you and I miss you.

To my pastor, the Rev. Dr. Cynthia Hale, you are indeed my spiritual mentor. Not only do you preach the gospel of Christ, but you live it! You left an enormous impact on my life and I am so thankful that you continue to allow God to use you to bless all those that are fortunate to come across your path. May God continue to bless you.

To my Children, Lance, Chris, Kari, Dana, Aminah and Aishah, and to my grandchildren, Chris, Keone, Aaron, Noah, Heaven, Nia, Tahie, Ja'el, Jasmine, Justin, Amariah, Serenity and Lindsay, I will continue to strive for greatness so that I may always be an example for you to follow. I am blessed to have you all in my life. I love you all!

To my sisters, Rhonda, Cheryl, and Marline, thank you for being my sisters not only in blood, but in Christ. For that, I am forever grateful to have the best prayer partners and warriors I could ever ask God for! May God continue to bless all that you do, I love you.

To My Force of Friendship Sisters, thank you for your support, friendship and love. Thank you for your belief in me and your continued encouragement. I love you with the love of Christ!

Stephanie, thank, you for allowing God to use your gifts and your talents to bring this book to life. Your friendship has been a blessing!

Lacie, your creative ability melts my heart. Thank you for using your gift to create this amazing book cover!

Thank you, Tanisha for taking this fantastic photograph.

WHY ARE YOU SITTING ON
YOUR GREATNESS?

CHAPTER 1

WHY ARE YOU SITTING ON YOUR GREATNESS?

ARE YOU ALLOWING GOD TO INSTRUCT AND DIRECT YOU TO YOUR GREATNESS?

Psalm 32:8 says, "God will instruct us and teach us the way to go. He will watch over us and guide us with His eyes!"

There were so many times when I thought I could make it on my own, only to find myself in a big mess because I did not allow God to instruct me. I wanted things in my own time, not in God's time. It is so easy to follow what we think is the right way to go or to take advice from those that we think are the right people, instead of seeking God's will. What I have come to realize is that God's way is always better. God needs us to be at a point where we are open to allowing Him to instruct and guide us. There is nothing like being watched over and guided by the eyes of God. Many people never see their dreams become a reality because they are taking instructions from the wrong people. Be mindful of your circle of influence! We can never go wrong, and we can always be confident when we allow God to do what He does best. He will always guide us in the direction of His Will!

"Those that trust in, rely on and confidently lean on the Lord shall be compassed with mercy and with His loving-kindness." Psalm 32:11

Decide today that you will not sit on your greatness.

Do you feel like you have the guidance you need to achieve your dreams?

Do you take advice from the wrong people?

Are you afraid to admit it because they are your (so-called) friends?

Can you recall where you have gone wrong by not allowing God to instruct you?

Do you find it hard to trust God because you feel like He has not come through for you in the past?

WHY ARE YOU SITTING ON YOUR GREATNESS?

ARE YOU ALLOWING OTHERS TO STEAL YOUR GREATNESS?

One of the greatest gifts God has given us is the power of our words. When we allow others to speak words that seal our greatness, we have given them our power! It is so important for us to speak up against those negative people and their words. We often allow them to take up space in our minds and that is when we are headed down the road of defeat. Some people are so miserable about their own lives they cannot see or do not want to see the greatness in you, so what do they do? They come to tear down your dreams! What you have to do is be determined not to allow anyone to steal your dreams and be willing to fight to protect them with every fiber of your being.

Some people will never realize their own greatness because they continue to allow others to steal it and, the sad part is, they die taking their greatness to the grave, never tapping into it and if you are not careful, they will take yours with them. Know that you are born with greatness inside of you!

Decide today that you will not sit on your greatness!

Are you allowing others to steal your greatness?

Is your greatness important to you?

Do you speak words of greatness into your life every day?

Do you feel defeated by the words of others?

WHY ARE YOU SITTING ON YOUR GREATNESS?

ARE YOU SCARED OF YOUR GREATNESS?

2 Timothy 1:7 tells us that God has not given us the spirit of fear but power, love, and self-discipline!

"TAKE CONTROL OF YOUR GREATNESS!"

The reason most people find it challenging to overcome their weaknesses and their fears, is because our minds are the battlefield for the enemies' tactics, which are directed towards our thinking. Our thoughts are like a computer and your subconscious mind is the storage drive which holds all the information you feed it. It stays there until you need it. For example, when we speak and think doubt, fear, lack, comparing ourselves with others, your computer does what you tell it to do. It will always agree with you! Isaiah 55:11 tells us, "That my words that go out of my mouth will not return to me empty, but they will accomplish what I send them out to do." As well as Proverbs 18:21 lets us know that "There is life and death in the power of the tongue."

My question to you, are you speaking untruths into your life? "Nobody likes me", "I am shy", "that may work for you because you are great with people, but I don't like people", "I am too fat", "I am lazy", "I am too scared," the list goes on and on. These two words "I am" are very powerful because whatever you put after them shapes who you are! God tells us to speak truth into our lives, which comes from His word. Phil 4:13 says, "We can do ALL THINGS through Christ who strengthens us," Phil 4:19 NIV says "My God will meet all my needs according to His glorious riches in Christ Jesus." Matt 7:7 says, "Ask, and it will be given to you." What is God saying? Whatever you need, ask ME, but there is a requirement. You must believe that I can do it! Fear will bring us down; faith is the key that will take us to higher heights.

I believe the only way we can take control of our fears is to believe in the power of Jesus Christ and His word!

Decide today that you will not sit on your greatness!

Who do you believe you are?

Do you see yourself as God sees you?

Do you fear being great?

What are you allowing to hold you back?

Do you have friends that believe you deserve the best that God has to offer you?

WHY ARE YOU SITTING ON YOUR GREATNESS?

ARE YOU SEEKING GOD FOR YOUR GREATNESS?

Matthew 6:33 tells us, "Seek first the kingdom of God and His righteousness and all these things will be given to you"!

I know in my life there have been times when I have attempted to do things my way without seeking God for his guidance, thinking I had it all under control only to find myself right where God needed me to be, asking Him for help. I can remember a time when I was going after a huge goal and I needed the support and help of one of my team members, I thought I heard the voice of the Lord say "ask," and so I did; and she said no! I was so devastated by her response, but then immediately I heard the voice of God say, "I did not tell you to ask her, I said ask ME!" What I realized is that I had allowed myself to think I heard God's voice saying ask her but she was not the one who could help me in achieving my goal, only God could do that. It was at that moment that I really understood how important it is to seek God and only God for what you want and need!

Decide today that you will not sit on your greatness!

What are you seeking God for?

Have there been times when you know you should have asked God for something, but you asked man instead?

Do you find yourself seeking others for help before you go to God?

What are your regrets about not going to God first?

WHY ARE YOU SITTING ON YOUR GREATNESS?

ARE YOU SPEAKING GREATNESS INTO YOUR LIFE DAILY?

It is important to speak words that empower you daily! People are accustomed to saying the wrong things, like "it's ok that things did not go the way intended", and they wonder why their dreams are not coming true. It is because they have not learned how to speak words that empower their lives. In the word of God, He shows us how we should be thinking, speaking, and believing. All of His promises are "yes", and all we need to do is speak it and believe it. We must also stop allowing others to speak negative things into our lives - we do not have to accept the negative thoughts of others! It is none of our business what others think of us, but it is our business what we think of ourselves. You want your words and your good deeds to glorify God! (Mathew 5:16) Be mindful of the words you speak make sure you speak words of power; they build your confidence and when you build your confidence you can conquer anything!

Decide today that you will not sit on your greatness!

Are you speaking words that empower you?

Are you letting others speak negative words to you?

What are you doing to help build your confidence?

Are you concerned what others think about you?

WHY ARE YOU SITTING ON YOUR GREATNESS?

ARE YOU TURNING TO GOD AND GODLY PEOPLE FOR HELP WHEN YOU ARE FACED WITH DIFFICULT LIFE DECISIONS?

There have been many times in my life that I can admit to not seeking guidance from God when faced with a crisis. I am going to share a time when, thankfully, I was wise enough to seek the help from God to save a life.

My youngest daughter had become pregnant when she was 14 years old. Needless to say, I was devastated! I remember God saying to me, "dare not you stand in judgment for you have stood here!" I too became pregnant very young. I was just 16 years old when I became pregnant with my oldest son. Sometimes God has to remind us of our own shortcomings to make sure we do not judge others. As a new believer, I was not sure what to do in this situation. Many said that she was just too young to have this baby and that she should get an abortion. Completely lost and feeling hopeless I made an appointment at the abortion clinic. I remember crying out to God for Him to tell me what to do. I asked Him to please show His presence because I needed His guidance and He showed up! They took my daughter to the back to do the procedure but shortly after, the doctor came out to talk to me. He said that if they performed the procedure it would cause her complications in the future and to come back in the morning to see the specialist. I knew right away that God was telling me not to go through with it. Still uncertain and questioning what I thought was the voice of God, I was wise enough to seek out Godly wisdom for confirmation. I called a family friend who also happened to be a pastor and a doctor. What I loved most about the conversation with her, was she was never judgmental. She was kind and loving and spoke with such gentleness. Her voice was soothing and I could feel the presence of God speaking through her. She was so calming at such a critical time in my life. She told me how God felt about everything in such a way that I knew for sure I had indeed made the right decision on that day. Nine months later my daughter gave birth to a beautiful, healthy baby boy. Today he is doing amazing things with the life that God spared on that day 22 years ago!

I believe that stepping into your greatness requires that you seek God at all times and that you walk by faith - especially when you are faced with a serious crisis and making the most difficult decisions in life. Let God direct you to those people that will give you Godly advice when you are not sure of what to do. I realized that I did have the faith I needed to trust God in my situation.

My grandson has grown up to be a great young man and just think, if I had operated in fear instead of faith, I would have missed a huge blessing! Had we not listened to the voice of God my grandson would not be here today to become a fire fighter. I am so happy that I cried out to God instead of listening to the world.

Decide today that you will not sit on your greatness!

Have there been times when you have allowed the world to advise you on what to do in situations instead of seeking God and Godly council?

If so, how did it turn out?

Are you allowing fear to stop you or faith to propel you?

Do you believe that it is important to have faith in God and allow Him to guide you into your greatness?

WHY ARE YOU SITTING ON YOUR GREATNESS?

ARE YOU WILLING TO STAND UP FOR YOUR GREATNESS?

It is imperative to stand up for your greatness. You have to be willing to fight for it. Others will not fight for your greatness that is something you have to do. When you decide to fight for it you create a path that will lead you straight to your greatness. We must stop avoiding our greatness. How do we avoid our greatness? We do that by allowing things that take up our time so that we no longer have the time to focus on what we need to be doing so our greatness will unfold. We cannot discover our greatness when we focus on all the things that pull us away from it. There is no time for making excuses and complaining about why we are not where we want to be in life. It is time to give it all we have to make our dreams come true, but we must stand up for our greatness and stop letting others interfere with our fight for greatness!

Decide today that you will not sit on your greatness!

Are you standing up for your greatness?

What are the things you are doing to keep you from your greatness?

Who is interfering in your fight for greatness?

Are you ready to give all you have for your greatness?

Do you believe that your dreams can come true?

WHY ARE YOU SITTING ON YOUR GREATNESS?

ARE YOU INTENTIONAL ABOUT YOUR GREATNESS?

To see your greatness become a reality, you must become intentional about it. Your greatness will not happen by accident.

Those who have achieved greatness were very intentional about the dreams and goals that they set for themselves. Alex Pineda said, "every year people set new goals based on emotions and then 'hope' that it will be the year they will accomplish them, but then the emotions die down and the year goes by and they are either in the same position or a worse one!"

You have to be intentional about your plan and then put it into action! Being intentional means getting things done on purpose and being deliberate about it. Most people find it hard to achieve their greatness because they are not willing to be intentional about their dreams and accomplishing their goals. That is the key to achieving your greatness. Decide today that you are going to be intentional.

Decide today that you will not sit on your greatness!

What is stopping you from being intentional about your greatness?

Are you one of those people who are just sitting around hoping your greatness will show up?

Do you set goals every year but can't understand why they are not being accomplished?

Are you willing to be intentional about your dream and goals?

WHY ARE YOU SITTING ON YOUR GREATNESS?

CHAPTER 2

WHY ARE YOU SITTING ON YOUR GREATNESS?

CONSISTENCY IS KEY!

To be consistent means to fully dedicate yourself entirely to a task, activity or goal. There is power in our consistency. The biggest challenge in discovering our greatness is our inability to stay consistent. I know that when I make up my mind to do something, I can do it, but only when I am consistent will I see success. One of my biggest challenges has been staying consistent in my weight loss journey. I know that my biggest demon is SUGAR! If I am not strong and lack discipline, sugar will take away my power to be consistent with losing weight. It affects my health in a negative way. It takes away my energy and gives me anxiety. When I am not consistent with my health, I am not giving myself a fighting chance to be successful in any area of my life.

Here are some of things we need to do daily to help us to be consistent:
- Keep your eyes on the goal.
- Remind yourself daily why you are doing what you are doing.
- Keep images in front of you to remind you of what your success is going to look like when you finish your goal.
- Share with those that you know will help you to stay on track.
- Create a daily journal about your consistency.

Decide today that you will not sit on your greatness!

What keeps you from being consistent?

In your mind, what does consistency look like?

Are you serious about being consistent?

What benefits do you see in being consistent?

Are you willing to take the necessary step to be consistent?

WHY ARE YOU SITTING ON
YOUR GREATNESS?

CHAPTER 3

WHY ARE YOU SITTING ON YOUR GREATNESS?

DID YOU KNOW THAT THE DEVIL CANNOT WIN WHEN YOU HAVE A PROMISE FROM GOD?

How many times have you heard people make this comment, "the Devil is busy!" Each time I hear this I say to myself, "my God is bigger than anything that the devil can bring!"

There are thousands of promises in God's word. These promises give me complete confidence that I have the victory over the enemy. I can remember when my husband was fired from his job unlawfully and it put a huge strain on us financially. I knew then that I had to stand on the promises of God. How many of you know that when you decide to stand on God's promises it only gets harder? We had to fight hard to get my husband's job back. After going back and forth through mediation with the company he worked for it was finally time to present his case, but the person that was over his case moved on to a new job. This meant the new person who took over his case had to start from the beginning! This was extremely frustrating for my husband. After two long years of mediation we finally got a hearing date. I can remember my husband feeling very skeptical about the outcome and I had to remind him that the battle was not his but the Lord's! After his case was presented they told us that it would take 3 months before we would hear anything back about the case. Three months passed and one day I heard my husband yell, "hallelujah" at the top of his lungs. If you know my husband, Neil, then you know that he is a man of very few words. Hearing him yell "hallelujah" was shocking! I ran downstairs to see what was going on and he told me that they finally awarded him back his job along with all back pay and benefits! I believe that this is a perfect example that the devil cannot win when you believe God for his promises. We must always keep our eyes on God.

Decide today that you will not sit on your greatness!

Do you trust the promises of God, even when the outcome looks dim?

Do you focus more on the problem or the promise?

Do you lack belief in God's promises?

Do you know what it takes to receive the promises of God?

WHY ARE YOU SITTING ON YOUR GREATNESS?

DID YOU KNOW THAT YOUR IDENTITY IS IN CHRIST?

I had to learn who I was in Christ and that I was not average. I had to accept the greatness that God gave me. My power to be great never came from man, only God! I can remember Dr. Regina Stewart preaching a sermon entitled, "Nobody Wants to be Average!" She said, "people do not want to invest in being average! Average does not place demands on you, and it does not call you to the excellence in Christ. Leaving Christ out of the equation, you will only come up with nothing!" Hearing that made me think, why would I want to go back to being average when I can be great in Christ? I have decided to be extraordinary in Christ!

Decide today that you will not sit on your greatness!

Are you living an average life?

Do you know your true identity in Christ?

Do you desire to live an extraordinary life?

Do you find it easy to go back to what you know?

WHY ARE YOU SITTING ON YOUR GREATNESS?

DO NOT ALLOW YOUR HURT FROM OTHERS TO KEEP YOU FROM GOD'S BLESSINGS!

I can relate to this! I am the kind of person that loves hard. I found so many times I allowed myself to become bitter and angry because of something someone did to hurt me when all I did was show them love. I dwelt in my pain instead of healing and moving on. I would often ask myself, "what could I have done differently?" I had to permit myself to move on from all those bad feelings. Life is too short to focus on all the hurt and pain that it brings! We need to stay in tune with God in order to keep our love and light from diminishing once we come in contact with people who hurt us.

I remember God asking, "Nora, do you want people to bless and love you who do not desire to?" My answer to Him was, "no Lord, for my greatest blessings come from you!" From that day forward I decided to keep my eyes on Him and not allow my hurt from others to keep me from my greatness!

Decide today that you will not sit on your greatness!

Are you allowing your hurts from others to keep you from your greatness?

Are you willing to change your thoughts about your pain?

Do you realize that your greatest blessings come from God and not man?

Do you realize you must seek God at all times?

WHY ARE YOU SITTING ON YOUR GREATNESS?

DO YOU BELIEVE IN THE GREATNESS OF JESUS?

Recently I heard Bishop Mark Tolbert preach these words, "we have to prove that we have faith, we have to say it with our mouth before we can see it. It does not matter if we do not see it, the only thing that matters is that we believe God!" Your faith should be recognized! Has Jesus seen your faith recently?

Jesus can make a way out of no way if we believe Him. If you let the devil convince us that there is no power in the name of Jesus than your faith needs a tune up.

Mathew 9: 20-22 tells us of a woman with issued of blood. *"And behold, a woman who had suffered from the flow of blood for twelve years came up behind Him and touched the hem of His garment. For she kept saying to herself, If I only touch the hem of His garment I shall be healed. Jesus turned around and seeing her, He then said, Take courage, daughter! Your faith has made you well. And at once the woman was healed!"* It was her faith that healed her. The very fact that she believed if she could just touch His garment she would instantly be healed. It was her faith in the power of Jesus greatness.

Decide today that you will not sit on your greatness.

Do you have faith in the power of Jesus?

Does your faith need a tune up?

What do you think about the woman with the issue of blood?

Do you have confidence in your greatness?

WHY ARE YOU SITTING ON YOUR GREATNESS?

DO YOU SPEND MORE TIME ON YOUR INABILITIES OR YOUR GREATNESS?

Focusing on your abilities and not your inabilities is critical. I would often focus on what I could not do instead of what I was capable of doing. I think a lot of it had to do with the kind of people I was allowing myself to associate with, people who were small thinkers, negative thinkers, people who did not see life's possibilities for themselves. I eventually felt myself becoming one of them. I had to decide to change my circle of friends so I could be focus on my gifts and see my abilities instead of being distracted by what I could not see!

Time waits for no one; it keeps moving whether you are ready or not! I love what Dr. Martin Luther King Jr. said, that "not everyone could be famous, but everyone can be great, because your service determines your greatness!" Dr. King did not spend time focusing on his inabilities he spent his time focusing on his ability to serve others and making a difference in the world.

Decide today that you will not sit on your greatness!

What do you see, your inabilities or your abilities?

What does your circle of friends look like?

Do you have faith in your abilities?

Are you willing to embrace your abilities?

WHY ARE YOU SITTING ON YOUR GREATNESS?

DO NOT BE WILLING TO QUIT ON YOUR GREATNESS!

How many times in life were we willing to quit when life threw us a curve ball without thinking that it was possibly just a test? I believe that is Gods' way of seeing if we really want what we say we want and if we are willing to fight for it. I heard something from a little Jamaican boy, he said that, "you must fight for what you want because what you want will not fight for you!" I find that people give up too quickly and miss out on all that life has in store for them. They seem to be ok with life passing them by without even taking a second thought about their experience being any different. It is so crucial for us to move past all the naysayers who only can see the glass half full, it is vital always to be moving towards your greatness no matter what it looks like know that greatness awaits you on the other side.

Decide today that you will not sit on your greatness!

Are you listening to the naysayers about life?

Are you willing to quit on your dreams?

Do you have any dreams?

Are you on track for your Dreams?

How many times have you been thrown, a curve ball?

WHY ARE YOU SITTING ON YOUR GREATNESS?

DO NOT GET CAUGHT UP IN YOUR CIRCUMSTANCES!

One of the quotes I love to share with people is "your circumstances do not determine your destiny." I believe when we focus on our circumstances, we cannot see the possibilities that God has for us. Our circumstances are only temporary, but the more you focus on them the more permanent they seem to become. What you feed lives and what you starve dies. That is what we must do to our circumstances, starve them. You may be asking how can you do that? Below is a list of ways on how to stave your circumstances:

- Stop talking about them.
- Watch your circle of influences (friends, family or anyone that is negative, social media, television etc!)
- See your possibilities.
- Find Scriptures that Speak life into your life daily.
- Make a plan to change your circumstances.
- Read books that inspire you and show you how to see God working things out.
- Write a daily affirmation. For example, Isaiah 55:11 *"God tell us that our words will not return to us void."* That means if you speak positively about the thing you want to become a reality in your life, it will happen.

Decide today that you will not sit on your greatness!

How do you look at your circumstances?

What are you willing to do to change your current circumstances?

Who are you hanging around that could influence your thinking about your circumstances?

Do you see the problems in your life, or the possibilities?

WHY ARE YOU SITTING ON
YOUR GREATNESS?

CHAPTER 4

WHY ARE YOU SITTING ON YOUR GREATNESS?

EVERY GREAT DREAM STARTS WITH A SMALL VISION!

The thing I admire most about dreams is that they are free to see and possible to achieve but only if you believe.

Genesis 1:1-6, "In the Beginning, God created (prepared, formed & fashioned) the heavens and the earth. The earth was without form, an empty waste. Darkness was upon the face of the great deep. The Spirit of God was moving (hovering & brooding) over the waters, and then God said, let there be light, and then there was light and God saw that the light was good (suitable, pleasant) and He approved it and separated the light from the darkness and God called the light Day and the darkness He called Night and there was evening and there was morning, one day!"

As I thought about this chapter, I asked God to direct me. I believe in the beginning it started small, then God began to form the greatness, and after He created everything, He created us, one of His greatest masterpieces! That is how dreams are formulated. They start out small and as we continue to believe in them and nurture them, they become a great reality. I think the downfall for most people is that they think that if the dream does not look significant to them, it must not be a good dream. I believe that God blesses us with ideas (our dreams, big and small), but it is our responsibility to take small ideas and create great, big dreams.

Psalm 37:4 "If you delight yourself in the Lord; He will give you the desires of your Heart"! Your Desires Are Your Dreams!

Decide today that you will not sit on your greatness!

Do you feel confident that your small dreams will become a big reality?

Do you believe in your dreams?

How do you nurture your dreams?

WHY ARE YOU SITTING ON YOUR GREATNESS?

EXCUSES ARE THE LIES WE TELL OURSELVES!

I have found is that it is extremely easy for people to convince themselves not to do the things they need to do to live successful and healthy lives. They are more comfortable with making excuses about why they are not willing to do what needs to be done. What they fail to realize is, they just told themselves a lie to make themselves feel better about wanting to live an average life. God did not call us to be average, He called us to be Great!

I was recently speaking to a woman that I was coaching and she said, "I am ending my coaching time because I have not been willing to do what I need to do." She then ended her session by saying, "but the goal has not changed!" My response to her was, "you just told yourself a lie because the goal has changed! If you are not doing what you need to do to make the goal a reality; then the goal has changed!"

We convince ourselves so that we feel better about what we are not willing to do, or we simply blame others. I believe this is why there are so few successful people at the top. Only 2% of people reach their level of desired success. I think it is because those 2% are not willing to allow life's issues to stop them. They refuse to sell themselves excuses. They have learned to push back and deal with whatever life brings their way and stay focused on the main thing. They are relentless about their dreams, and they are so committed that nothing or no one will get in the way of the visions given to them by God. They realize that when life hits, they have to handle it, but they will not let it stop them. It just amazes me how many of us make so many excuses about why we do not do what we need to do and how many of us allow life's issues to stop us from reaching our goals.

Recently my husband was talking to a family member and mentioned that he needed to lose weight. His response was that he was not willing to lose the weight if it meant he had to stop eating red meat because he loves steak. I said, "wow he just used the meat as an excuse!" He told himself the lie that steak was just too good to let go of just to make himself feel better about the fact that he was not willing to make the lifestyle change to lose the weight. It is crucial that we are always honest with ourselves about what we are willing or unwilling to do to make our dreams become a reality in our lives.

God has great and mighty things for us, but they are all just one decision away. All we have to do is be honest with ourselves!

Decide today that you will not sit on your greatness!

What excuses are you telling yourself?

What do you need to do to make that changed in your life?

Are you willing to go above and beyond to fulfill your dreams?

Are you an excuse maker?

What can you do to help yourself recognize when you are making an excuse?

WHY ARE YOU SITTING ON YOUR GREATNESS?

EMBRACE YOUR GREATNESS!

To embrace our greatness, we have to hold fast to the power of God that is inside of us. I believe that when we realize we were created for greatness, it is easier to embrace our greatness. Embracing our greatness helps us to see the importance of protecting it and not allowing others to steal it. The dictionaries definition of the word embrace is, "to accept, believe, change willingly, and enthusiastically, wholeheartedly, take to one's heart, with open arms." Wow, this is so powerful! When you embrace your greatness, you can see all the potential and the possibilities God has for you.

Decide today that you will not sit on your greatness!

Do you feel like you are embracing your greatness?

What do you need to do to embrace your greatness?

What does your greatness look like to you?

Are you allowing others to steal your greatness?

If so, what do you plan to do to change that?

WHY ARE YOU SITTING ON
YOUR GREATNESS?

CHAPTER 5

WHY ARE YOU SITTING ON YOUR GREATNESS?

GOD DESIGNED ME FOR GREATNESS!

1 Peter 2:9, "But you are a chosen race, a royal priesthood, a holy nation, a people for His own possession, that you may proclaim the excellencies of him who called you out of darkness into his marvelous light!"

Genesis 12:2, "And I will make of you a great nation, and I will bless you and make your name great so that you will be a blessing!"

These scriptures are telling us that God has designed us with greatness in mind; all we have to do is walk in it. We have to be careful not to allow what others do not see in us and stay focus on what we see.

Crisette Ellis, a girlfriend of mine, says, "You have to dare to see what we do not see. If you do not see greatness, then greatness will not appear!" I know I have been chosen for greatness, and I have decided to step in it!

Decide today that you will not sit on your greatness!

Do you believe God designed you for greatness?

Are you allowing others to determine your greatness?

Do you find it hard to see your greatness?

Do you believe you are chosen?

WHY ARE YOU SITTING ON YOUR GREATNESS?

GOD DID NOT WAKE ME UP TO SIT ON MY GREATNESS!

Ephesians 3:20 "Now to Him who can do far more abundantly beyond all that we ask or think, according to the power (Greatness) that works within us."

This scripture speaks volumes to me. It allows me to see the importance of not sitting on my greatness - that every morning God wakes me up is another opportunity for me to do great and mighty things with my life. God did not give me these gifts for me to sit on them; I must use them! I have to trust His plans for my life. He tells me in Jeremiah 29:11 that He *"...knows the plans I have for you, plans to give you hope and a future..."* It just cannot get any better than that! I have learned to put my trust in God's plans for my life and not in the intentions of others. We often trust the plans that others have for us, but those plans are not guaranteed. I had to learn to trust how God sees me and His plans for my life. The bottom line is others do not wake us up to fulfill our greatness. God does!

Decide today that you will not sit on your greatness!

Who are you trusting with your life?

Are waking up and sitting on your greatness?

Are you more concerned with the plans that others have for you?

Do you trust Gods plans for your life?

Are you willing to step into your greatness?

WHY ARE YOU SITTING ON YOUR GREATNESS?

GOD WANTS YOU TO SUCCEED!

2 Chronicles 31:32 "He sought his God and worked wholeheartedly... so he prospered."

God wants you to succeed, but you have to do certain things. You have to set dreams then work toward them one priority at a time. Most ideas fail for one reason - broken focus. Avoid distractions.

James 1:8, "A double-minded woman is unstable. In all her ways and can expect nothing from God."

Write down your plans and establish deadlines. Most people do not plan to fail, they fail to plan. Make a detailed list of daily activities and make a checklist! Above all, guard and prioritize your time. *"Make the most out of every chance you get" (Ephesians 5:16 TM).* Visualize yourself accomplishing your goals and attaining your dreams. Talk and think successfully like Moses did. Moses led God's people through the Red Sea successfully because "He kept his eyes on God! God kept Moses going in the right direction even when he could not see it. *"A wise woman will hear and increase in her learning" (Proverbs 1:5 NAS)*

If you will pay more for a good meal than a good book that means you value your stomach more than your mind. We should observe, read and grow. Create a circle of confidence around you. You will not experience God's success for you while you are talking defeat or allowing others to talk defeat around you. Do not rehearse your mistakes, which only reinforce your doubt. Remind yourself that your sufficiency is of God (2Co 3:5). With God as your partner, your success is guaranteed! It is essential to help others become successful. Know that *"whatever good we do to help others we will receive the same from the Lord!" (Ephesians 6:8).* That means conquering self-centeredness. It is a team effort, not an I effort. Putting God first is most important. You are His child and He desires for you to succeed. What father would not?

It is essential to deepen our relationship with God, this reassures us that when we ask for anything in his name, it will be done unto us!

Decide today that you will not sit on your greatness!

Do you know God wants you to succeed?

Are you clear about your dreams?

Do you see yourself achieving your dreams?

Are you taking God as your business partner?

Are you focusing on the words you speak?

WHY ARE YOU SITTING ON YOUR GREATNESS?

GOD'S CREATIVE ABILITY!

God made man the only being in the universe that can speak. I know a parrot can repeat phrases, but that is just talking, not communicating. Has it ever occurred to you why man is the only being with the power to communicate verbally? There is such a remarkable potential and power in our words and our ability to express them. Speaking words releases God's creative energy and strength. Animals do not possess this power and ability, but you and I have been created with the ability to speak and God said, "I will create whatever you utter with your lips."

He said, "I create the fruit of the lips, the utterance of the lips." Man can create whatever he speaks. God will give you whatever you dare to confess. Stop saying things like, "I hope I am going to be successful" or "I hope that my situation will change" or "I hope I can one day buy a house." Instead, start confessing with your mouth what you are seeking from God. Learn to speak those things that are not as though they are. The power is in your confession. Do not look at what you see, look far beyond that because your destiny is in God's hands and your mouth.

Decide today that you will not sit on your greatness!

Do you believe in God's ability?

Do you believe in your ability to speak greatness into your life?

Do you realize how remarkable you are?

Did you know that there is power in your confessions?

WHY ARE YOU SITTING ON YOUR GREATNESS?

GOD NEVER FORGETS DETAILS AND NOTHING SLIPS THROUGH THE CRACKS!

When I think of this statement, it reminds me of something my sister Cheryl told me. She said, "God always remembers the things we do for Him and when we least expect it, He will reach back into His bag of blessings and pull out a blessing for us!" This really blessed me! Never feel like God has forgotten about you because He never forgets the details of our lives. God pays close attention to each little detail; nothing slips through the cracks.

I can remember a situation I was in and it was one that only God could fix. I remember God saying these exact words to me, He said, "it's all right I fixed it" yet here I was, overthinking and crying and honestly wondering If God had forgotten about me. When God came to me with those words, I knew right then and there that He had not forgotten about me and that He worked out the details of my situation and my prayers had not slipped through the cracks. My God was taking care of business.

He is the only one that can handle any and every situation that may come up in our lives. The key is to remember that God never forgets the details of our lives and that no prayer or cry for help ever slips through the cracks!

Philippians 4:19 says, *"and this same God who takes care of me, will supply all of your needs from His glorious riches which have been given to us in Christ Jesus."*

Deuteronomy 31:6 says, *"Be strong and courageous. Do not be afraid or terrified because of them, for the Lord your God goes with you; He will never leave you nor forsake you!"*

Decide today that you will not sit on your greatness!

Do you feel like God has forgotten the details of your life?

Do you feel like He has allowed things to slip through the cracks?

Are you sharing with God the hidden things in your heart (even though He already knows)?

Are you willing to trust Him through the processes?

Are you paying attention to those who cannot take you where you want to go or are paying attention to God?

WHY ARE YOU SITTING ON YOUR GREATNESS?

GOD'S TIMING IS ALWAYS RIGHT!

I can recall being frustrated at times in my life waiting on God. I had to learn that God's timing is always best, but I had to find that out the hard way, as most people do! We live in a microwave wave society. We want it now or even yesterday, but it just does not work that way with God. God knows our beginning and our end, and because God knows what is best for us it is so important to wait on His timing. My sister taught me something many years ago, and I still use it to this day. When I want something, l look up to heaven, and I say, "God if this is Your will for me open every door. If not, close every door and I am totally fine with it!"

I can remember when we wanted to refinance our home because we added a second mortgage. This was a bad mistake and the interest rate was awful. After many years we received an offered to refinance our home. At the time we thought it was a good idea because we wanted to pay off the second mortgage. I prayed before going to the mortgage company and they came back and told us that everything looked good. Two days before we were supposed to close, they came back and said "no!" I could remember being so upset, but then I heard this soft voice saying to me, "you said if that was not My will to close the door!" I knew it was God and I said, "yes Lord, You are right!" We realized that if we were approved, we would have made another bad mistake operating on our time and not God's time. God knows our beginning and our end. His timing is so important. We must listen to Him when He guides us!

In the book of Psalms 32:8 God says, *"I instruct and teach you the way you should go, I will counsel you, I watch over you, I will guide you with my eyes!"* God's timing is always best!

Decide today that you will not sit on your greatness!

How do you feel about God's timing?

Are you willing to wait on Him?

Have you been doing things your way and in your time?

Are you willing to allow God to instruct you?

Do you have a problem waiting on God?

WHY ARE YOU SITTING ON YOUR GREATNESS?

GREATNESS ALWAYS MEETS GREATNESS!

Believing in yourself and in your abilities is essential to making things happen in your life and to embrace your greatness. Being great is not about the ego or selfishness. The path to greatness consists of having a strong and genuine desire, a purpose, as well as surrounding yourself with people who will help you endure as you walk through life. Greatness is not a one-time effort, it is a way of life!

William Shakespeare once said, "be not afraid of greatness. Some are born great, some achieve greatness, and others have greatness pushed upon them."

When I read this, it showed me that greatness always meets greatness. When you decide to be great and embrace your greatness you will attract great things and people. Make sure you are intentional about your greatness. Follow what God has to say and the way He wants you to go. God never makes a mistake. Everything He does is intentional.

Trust and believe in what God has to say, do not listen to the naysayers in your life. I can remember a woman telling me that I was not a good writer and that I would never be one. Just imagine if I listened to her, I would have never embraced my greatness and you would not be reading this book.

It does not matter what others have to say about you. It only matters what God says. Remember, greatness always meets greatness!

Decide today that you will not sit on your greatness!

Do you believe in your greatness?

Are you surrounding yourself with people who believe in your greatness?

Do you feel like you were born with greatness?

Are you afraid of greatness?

Are you willing to sacrifice for your greatness?

WHY ARE YOU SITTING ON YOUR GREATNESS?

GREATNESS COST AND THERE IS NO MARK DOWN!

I do not remember where I heard this quote, but when I heard it I loved it! "There is a cost for greatness! There is a price one must be willing to pay, and there is no avoiding payment. It will not be marked down because we refuse to pay the full price."

How do we pay for greatness? When we do the things that we need to do to develop our greatness it shows we are willing to pay the price for it. I want to encourage you to stay on your path to your greatness and never give up.

Here are a few things we need to do in order to develop our inner greatness:
- We have to be willing to seek God in everything we do.
- We have to be willing to do the work when we don't feel like it.
- We have to be willing to let go of negative people.
- We have to be willing to learn from our mistakes.
- We have to be willing to break out of our comfort zone.
- We have to be willing to continuously learn how to be and do better.
- Make yourself accountable to a mentor, someone who can help you when you get off track.

Decide today that you will not sit on your greatness!

Are you willing to pay the price for greatness?

Are you willing to change your bad habits for good ones to obtain your greatness?

Are you willing to let go of the relationships that are interfering with your greatness?

Are you willing to make the necessary sacrifices for your greatness?

Are you willing to learn from your mistakes?

WHY ARE YOU SITTING ON YOUR GREATNESS?

GREATNESS UNUSED IS UNCOMFORTABLE!

Sooner or later unused greatness becomes very uncomfortable because it keeps you in place of mediocrity and it causes you to settle for less than what you deserve. When we become uncomfortable, it should cause us to move beyond the place of mediocrity. Becoming complacent with where you are is a dangerous place to be! I believe that God has created us to be great and He allows things to happen to cause us to be uncomfortable. His intentions are to move us to the next level of greatness, but because He gives us free will, it is our choice to move to our next level of greatness or become complacent with where we are!

It is sad to see people not using their greatness and just allowing themselves to stay in this uncomfortable place of mediocrity. It hurts my heart to see them allowing their gifts to lay dormant! God has blessed us with so many gifts and it is a sin for us not to use them. We dishonor God when we do not use our gifts. It is important that we show God how much we appreciate Him. I think we spend too much time listening to people and not the one who can direct us into our greatness. Psalms 32:8 tells us that God will instruct us and show us the way to go; that He will watch over us and guide us with His eyes! We cannot ask for better guidance than that. I want you to step outside of your comfort zone and use your power to great!

Decide today that you will not sit on your greatness!

Are you allowing your greatness to lay dormant?

Are you uncomfortable with where you are?

Do you believe in your greatness?

Do you feel worthy of your greatness?

Do you allow others to direct your path instead of God?

WHY ARE YOU SITTING ON
YOUR GREATNESS?

CHAPTER 6

WHY ARE YOU SITTING ON YOUR GREATNESS?

HOW DO YOU SEE YOURSELF?

Often times we see ourselves the way others see us. This is why it is so important to only see ourselves the way God sees us! Psalms 139:14 tells us that we are fearfully and wonderfully made by God and God's work is wonderful. God does not take the time to make useless junk. Everything He makes is beautiful. We spend too much time listening to the wrong people and what they have to say about us. When people attempt to even think to speak negative words to you, stop them dead in their tracks. You must never accept anyone's negative perceptions of you and you must know that you are what God says you are - you are powerful, awesome, mighty, and great! You have to confess it!

Recite this affirmation our loud daily:
I am a woman of excellence and I will get the job done! I am a woman on a mission with passion and a vision. I love change in my life! I will go over, under and through any obstacles that get in my way. I will not tolerate self-pity, negativity or gossip from myself or others. I am energetic and enthusiastic and I turn excuses into reasons. I cannot be pitiful and powerful at the same time, so I choose to be powerful! I am a woman of excellence!

- Nora Shariff-Borden

Decide today that you will not sit on your greatness!

How do you see yourself?

Do you see yourself the way others see you?

Do you believe in your greatness?

Do you see yourself as a woman of excellence?

WHY ARE YOU SITTING ON YOUR GREATNESS?

HOW TO FORGIVE WHEN YOU HAVE BEEN HURT

This is a tough one because most people operate in their flesh when it comes to forgiveness. Most often when we are harboring feelings of unforgiveness, the person we are unable to forgive has already moved on or does not know they hurt us or that we feel that way. Unfortunately, these feelings will affect you mentally, emotionally and physically, causing it to become a danger to your health. Jesus teaches us that we must forgive 77 times 7! What I have come to learn is we have to seek God's help in forgiving. Each time He reminds us that He will always forgive us, so we must continually work on forgiving others. That does not mean we have to keep those people in our lives, but we need to forgive them to truly release them. You will feel so much better when you do!

Decide today that you will not sit on your greatness.

Are working on forgiving someone who has hurt you?

How do you process hurt?

Do you seek God's help with your feelings of pain?

Are ready to let those feelings go?

Is it hard for you to forgive?

WHY ARE YOU SITTING ON
YOUR GREATNESS?

CHAPTER 7

WHY ARE YOU SITTING ON YOUR GREATNESS?

I AM DOING MY BEST! I AM A WORK IN PROGRESS!

These words are nothing but an excuse! Excuses are the lies we tell ourselves when we want to keep on doing what we know is not right. God has not called us to make excuses, He has called us to a higher standard. We have to work hard every day to live up to the standards that God has placed upon our lives. We have not been created to live below but to live above. The next time you find yourself making the above statement stop and tell yourself you are capable of doing more than your best. Confess your greatness in Christ every day and walk in your greatness. Live out your greatness every day. Be who God has called you to be every day. Decide that you will believe who God says you are. Know that the spirit of the Lord goes before you making your way safe, joyous, and prosperous. His favor follows you wherever you may go. He shows and gives you favor in high places. Be grateful for all God has done and will do for you. It will help you to do better than "your best."

Decide today that you will not sit on your greatness!

Do you believe you are truly doing your best?

Is your best really good enough?

Is this an excuse you are telling yourself?

Do you believe you have the favor of God?

Are you willing to work on yourself every day?

WHY ARE YOU SITTING ON YOUR GREATNESS?

I OWE IT TO MYSELF!

I have come to realize I owe it to myself to always walk in my greatness. I believe that when I do, I honor God, for it is He that made me great and it is my responsibility to own it. We often allow others to tell us what we should or should not do and when we do that we have given them our power. Only God has control over our power. When we find ourselves in toxic relationships we are giving those people our power. There has to come a time when you must walk away. The more you go back, the more you give them control. I pray for God to show you who those persons are and to take the scales off your eyes so you can see the truth. The bottom line is you must see it for yourself. It took time for me to learn how but now it is easy for me to walk away from toxic people. When people show who they are, you must believe them. Especially if you asked God to show you. Believe Him when He shows you. Own your greatness and never give it away!

Decide today that you will not sit on your greatness.

Do you own your greatness?

Are you allowing others to steal your greatness?

Is your circle of influence positive or negative?

Do you realize you owe it to yourself to walk in your greatness?

Are you trusting God with your greatness?

WHY ARE YOU SITTING ON
YOUR GREATNESS?

CHAPTER 8

WHY ARE YOU SITTING ON YOUR GREATNESS?

LEARN HOW TO EMBRACE YOUR OWN GREATNESS!

The hardest thing for me to do for so long was to embrace my own greatness. I was so busy comparing myself to my girlfriends. They all had college degrees and I did not. I spent so much time focusing on them and what they possessed that I did not allow myself to embrace my own greatness.

It is so important to keep your eyes on God and what God has for you and not what you see in others. He has created us all with unique, individual gifts and what I had to learn was how to embrace what God has given me and run with it. My friends are powerful women yes, but guess what? So am I! I decided to change how I looked at my girlfriends and start to look at them as an inspiration and a good example and be happy they are in my circle of influence and to embrace my very own greatness.

Decide today that you will not sit on your greatness!

Are you embracing your own greatness or are you focusing on the greatness of others?

Do you compare yourself to others?

Do you have confidence in who you are?

Do you have friends who embrace your greatness?

How do you stay away from toxic people?

WHY ARE YOU SITTING ON YOUR GREATNESS?

LEARN HOW TO WAIT YOUR TURN!

One of the hardest things for me was waiting patiently for my turn to shine. You know how it is when we want it right now, waiting is not an option. When we do not wait, we find ourselves in a big mess. I learned over the years that waiting on God and His perfect timing is crucial. I learned a lot of hard lessons because I refused to wait patiently on God to grant me the things I wanted. We must be patient and have an attitude of gratitude while we are waiting on God or we will end up wanting what we want so badly that we convince ourselves that it was God speaking to us. We want to be certain that all of our blessings are directly from God. When we rush the process instead of patiently waiting for God we will most certainly fail. You will then hear God say, "I did not tell you to do that!" I am so glad that I learned how to wait on God. Isaiah 40:31 tells us that *"those who wait on the Lord shall renew their strength; they shall mount up on the wings of eagles; they shall run, and not be weary, and they shall walk and not grow faint."* God is clearly showing us the importance of waiting our turn.

Decide today that you will not sit on your greatness.

Do you find it hard to wait on God?

Do you find yourself in drama because you did not wait on God?

Do you think you hear God but are not sure?

Are you learning to wait for your turn?

WHY ARE YOU SITTING ON
YOUR GREATNESS?

CHAPTER 9

WHY ARE YOU SITTING ON YOUR GREATNESS?

MAKE SURE YOUR INTENTIONS ARE CLEAR!

Be open and allow opportunities to present themselves to you when things do not go as intended. Trust that God has your back and has better plans for your life! Despite how things may look or seem, use your energy on your faith in God and make sure that your intentions are crystal clear. When your intentions for your life are unclear you feel like you are walking in a fog and cannot see the road ahead. When we follow God's plans for our lives we come out on the other side of the mist where the sun is shining brightly and the road to success is clear allowing us to follow the directions of God! God's plans for us are always going to be greater than any plan we could ever have for ourselves. He desires that we become all that He has called us to be - powerful, mighty, great and nothing less! Make sure your intentions are always clear.

Decide today that you will not sit on your greatness!

Are your intentions for your life clear?

Do you follow God's will for your life?

Do you feel like you are in a fog?

Are you walking by faith?

WHY ARE YOU SITTING ON YOUR GREATNESS?

MAKING A DECISION TO WALK INTO YOUR GREATNESS NO MATTER WHAT LIFE THROWS YOUR WAY!

Deciding to walk in your greatness is not always the easiest thing to do, especially when life seems to take a turn for the worst. I was in the Apple Store looking to purchase a new Mac computer and I noticed the young salesman who was helping me only had one arm. After I made my purchase, I decided to ask him if he minded telling me what happen to his arm. He went on to share that 9 years ago he was a race car driver and one night he lost control of his car. It flipped over 10 times causing him to lose his arm. He was married with a 6-month-old son and his wife was a stay at home mom. After the accident left him out of work, he and his wife decided she would go back to work and he would stay home and take care of their baby. He shared that, with much determination, he learned how to change his son's diaper and how to completely care for him with just one arm! I believe that when he decided to stay home and take care of his son is when he realized he would not sit on his greatness! He said he was thankful that God saw fit to spare his life and allow him to be around to care for his child.

I believe that God wants us to see, in spite of what happens in our lives, we must still be willing to walk in our greatness! That is exactly what Widdy Michel did. Even though he experienced the trauma of losing his arm he still took on the task of caring for his son while his wife worked. Doing this, he realized his life was not over and there was so much more God had for him to do, including becoming an Apple Advisor. What an inspiration! He was determined to not allow his situation to affect his destiny. This story is a prime example of what it means to walk in your greatness.

Decide today that you will not sit on your greatness!

Are you walking in your greatness?

What is stopping you from walking in your greatness?

Are you determined to walk in your greatness?

Do you believe that your present situation does not determine your destiny?

What inspired you about Widdy's story?

WHY ARE YOU SITTING ON YOUR GREATNESS?

MOVING TOWARD YOUR GREATNESS!

It is so important to always to be moving in the direction of your greatness, even if you are moving at a slow pace because a slow progress is better than no progress. Dr. Albert Einstein said, "life is like riding a bicycle, to keep your balance; you must keep moving." Not moving towards your greatness causes you to become stuck and feeling paralyzed, but when you are moving and trusting God along your journey, He allows you to see all the great opportunities He has in store for you. When we do not move God will change our circumstances to force us to move and we will either look to God or look to people for help and people can fail you, God will not. Trust the plans God has for you, remember, they are always going to be great! This way of thinking keeps us moving towards our greatness.

Decide today that you will not sit on your greatness.

Do you feel like you are moving towards your greatness?

Has God had to close doors so that you will move towards your greatness?

Are you willing to go through the process to move towards your greatness?

Are you willing to trust Gods plans for your greatness?

Do you believe that greatness awaits you?

WHY ARE YOU SITTING ON
YOUR GREATNESS?

CHAPTER 10

WHY ARE YOU SITTING ON YOUR GREATNESS?

NEVER GIVE UP ON YOUR GREATNESS!

Greatness has nothing to do with where or how you grew up or your family background, it only has to do with your desire to walk in your own God given greatness. This greatness given to us by God allows to live a life full of purpose and passion. It causes us to work in our power every single day, constantly giving us the opportunity to walk in our own greatness. Greatness is not a one shot deal or something you just become. There has to be a lifelong and daily commitment because your greatness is a life long journey and not a destination you are racing to - it is a marathon. Your greatness is something you can NEVER GIVE UP ON. Albert Einstein said, "never give up on what you want to do. The person with big dreams is more powerful than the one with all the facts." It takes time to achieve all that you are destined to become, which is why it is crucial to fight for your greatness! There will be many obstacles placed in your path but as long as you overcome every single one and stay the course that God has set before you, one thing is for sure, it will pay off. Stay focused on your future and stop running back to your past. Leave your past self with your past habits, past people and places and run forward towards your greatness! We are born with greatness inside of us, but we must be willing to trust God and use the gifts that He has given us, for they are the very seeds to the fruit (abundance) we desire to bare! Our purpose is to walk in our own greatness!

Decide today that you will not sit on your greatness.

Have you given up on your greatness?

How hard are you willing to fight for your greatness?

Are you focused on your future or your past?

Are you committed to your journey?

WHY ARE YOU SITTING ON YOUR GREATNESS?

NO ONE CAN STEAL YOUR GREATNESS WITHOUT YOUR PERMISSION!

A lesson I was grateful to learn was that no one could steal my greatness unless I gave them the keys. I can think of the many times I willingly gave my greatness to people that did not deserve it. I would put all my trust in people and not in God, but that honestly landed me nowhere and only caused me to compare myself to others and I always came up short. I had to learn to put my trust in God. He has given me the power to be great in Him and I will never compare myself to anyone else again! I learned to walk in my greatness and in the Holy Spirit. I have decided to own it and never allow anyone to take it from me.

I have decided not to give my power away. I realize, *"greater is He that is in me than he that is in the world. (John4:4)* Which means because God resides inside of me, I have all the power I need to be great!

Decide today that you will not sit on your greatness.

Have you given away your greatness to undeserving people?

Do you believe in the greatness God has given you?

Is it important for you to own your greatness?

Do realize you have given others too much power in your life?

How can you take back your power?

WHY ARE YOU SITTING ON YOUR GREATNESS?

NOT PAYING ATTENTION TO GOD BUT BEING DECEIVED BY THE ENEMY!

It is essential for us to pay attention to what the Lord is telling us to do because the enemy is always looking for a way to trick us into thinking that his way is better than God's way. Even though we know that not to be true, we sometimes fall prey to his tricks. It is so important to focus on what the Lord has to say about our lives and not what others say or do. Many times we let the words or actions of others upset us or even tear us down. My thoughts around that is God has the last word. He knows when our hearts are pure and right, what we have to do is refuse to let the enemy deceive us. The Bible tells us that he comes to kill, steal, and destroy. Our job is to keep our eyes on God and His plans and His promises for our lives!

Decide today that you will not sit on your greatness!

Are you paying attention to God?

Are you being deceived by the enemy?

Are you allowing what others have to say about you take you off track?

Do you trust Gods plans for your life or are you falling prey to the enemy's plans?

WHY ARE YOU SITTING ON
YOUR GREATNESS?

CHAPTER 11

WHY ARE YOU SITTING ON YOUR GREATNESS?

SOMEONE WILL ALWAYS HAVE A PROBLEM WITH YOUR GREATNESS!

Know this, others will always have a problem with your greatness, because they see something in you that they wish they had in themselves. They will always have a problem with your greatness but not necessarily you personally. I never understood that until my friend Larry DiAngi explained it to me when I was going through a tough time in my life. I was hurt when I thought the people I had poured into had my back but later showed me their true self. I was shocked! When he poured that word into me, it gave me the power to get up and do what God had called me to do.

When we realize that people are not in charge of our destiny and that God is the one calling all the shots and when we believe in His Promises for our lives, nothing can interfere or stop the plans that He has for us. It does not matter if others have a problem with our greatness that is their problem and not ours.

Decide today that you will not sit on your greatness!

Are you concerned about what others think about you?

Do you realize that some people will always have a problem with your greatness?

Are you willing to look beyond those people and their thoughts of you?

Do you realize what others think about you is their problem and not yours?

Do you realize when you surround yourself with the right people great thing can and will happen?

WHY ARE YOU SITTING ON YOUR GREATNESS?

STOP ALLOWING OTHERS LACK OF BELIEF TO DETERMINE YOUR GREATNESS!

I know we can all relate to this one because there have been times in all of our lives where we have allowed the lack of belief of others to determine our greatness. The problem with this is that they do not see greatness for themselves, so they could not possibly see the greatness in you and want to see you succeed. They tear down your dreams and goals as a way to make themselves feel better about their own lack of greatness! What we have to do is be determined that we will not let their little thinking destroy our own ability to be great. We must know and own our power and eliminate those kinds of people from our lives. We must have the courage to stand up and fight for what we say we want.

There are steps we must take to live courageously:
- Confess to yourself every day that you are courageous.
- Close your eyes daily and see yourself where you want to be.
- See yourself as the powerful being that God created you to be.
- Find a great song that sets your soul on fire; music brings joy to the soul.
- Create a circle of influence of individuals you can reach out to
  for encouragement when you need it.

Decide today that you will not sit on your greatness.

Are you willing to work on your courage?

Have you evaluated your circle of influence lately?

Are you confessing what you want to happen in your life?

Do you see yourself as Powerful?

Do you see yourself where you want to be?

WHY ARE YOU SITTING ON
YOUR GREATNESS?

CHAPTER 12

WHY ARE YOU SITTING ON YOUR GREATNESS?

THE POWER TO BE GREAT RESIDES IN YOU. DO NOT LET OTHERS TAKE IT AWAY!

We often fail to realize that we all have the power to be great. The power to be great already resides inside of us! We have allowed others to speak death into our lives. Often times it happens as early as childhood and we grow up never realizing all of our greatness. Toxic people and their negativity are often the reason we lose our greatness. When we have toxic people around us who see nothing but the negative things that life has to offer them, they bring their toxic conversations and energies around us in an attempt to dim our light, but they can only do that if we to allow it.

I remember having a friend that was so negative and I did not like how I felt when I left her presence one day. I invited her to lunch and asked if I could have her permission to be honest. She gave me her permission and I told her how I felt. I told her that if we were going to continue to be friends that she had to stop being negative. She apologized and said she and no idea that she was that way and was so glad I shared my feelings with her. People cannot fix what they do not know is wrong. Many times, people just do not know about their toxic behavior because it has been a part of who they have been for so long and no one has ever brought it to their attention! It is our responsibility to tell people that we care about the truth so that they have the opportunity to fix the issue.

I shared this story with you because we often have these relationships with these kinds of people that cause us to unnecessarily doubt our greatness. Before we just cut them off, we need to give them the opportunity to change. We may be able to help them see the power that resides inside of them in the process of reclaiming their own light and greatness - which has always been there, it has just been dimmed!

Decide today that you will not sit on your greatness.

Do you believe greatness resides inside of you?

Do you have toxic people in your life?

Do you allow others to speak death into your life?

Do you have friends who support your greatness?

WHY ARE YOU SITTING ON YOUR GREATNESS?

THE ROAD TO GREATNESS IS NEVER EASY!

Steve Jobs said it best when he said, "have the courage to follow your heart and intuition; they somehow know what you truly want to become." I believe that intuition he is talking about is God!

We live in a confusing world. With so many options, choices and possibilities, we often find it hard to decide which direction to go. How do you know what your passion is if you have not found yourself? How do you accomplish your goals if you have yet to discover your deepest desires? The book of Psalms 37 says to *"delight yourself in the Lord and He will give you the desires of your heart."* Reading and following the word of God is the most promising way to identify who you are and get what you want. To Identify your gifts, you must do what you are good at and continuously work at it until you go from good to great. It may not be easy at first, but with hard work and dedication, it will become better with time. While on this journey to greatness, it is important to be thankful for what you already have and where you are. Have faith that the rest will come. Your greatness is already inside of you. You do not have to look for it.

Oprah hit the nail on the head when she said, "if you can't appreciate what you have, you'll never be able to capitalize on the opportunities life has given you. You'll never be one hundred percent happy. If you can show gratitude and appreciation for what you've got, you'll end up with more happiness and more success in the long run!" The road to greatness is never easy, but it is worth the journey!

Decide today that you will not sit on your greatness.

Did you expect your journey to be comfortable?

Do you appreciate what you have and where you are?

Are you happy with yourself?

How do you stay focused in the midst of chaos?

Are you grateful?

WHY ARE YOU SITTING ON YOUR GREATNESS?

THERE IS POWER IN THE NAME OF JESUS!

As a believer in Jesus Christ, I know that there is power in the name of Jesus! We have to know that He is the truth, the way and the life. *"No one comes to the Father except through me."* (John 14:6) We have to trust this power and that whatever we ask in the name of Jesus, it shall be done (according to His will). *"Jesus came and said to them, All authority in heaven and on earth has been, given to me!"* (Matthew 28:18) He has the power to change or fix anything that is happening in our lives. What we have to learn to do is call on Him in our time of need. There is nothing too big or small for God. When we "believe in the Name of Jesus," we are showing God that we believe in Him as our Lord and Savior and that all the power we need comes from Him.

There is Power in The Name of Jesus Christ!

Decide today that you will not sit on your greatness.

Do you believe in the power of the name Jesus Christ?

Do you believe that He can fix anything going on in your life?

Have you learned to call on him in your time of need?

How meaningful is your relationship with Jesus?

WHY ARE YOU SITTING ON
YOUR GREATNESS?

CHAPTER 13

WHY ARE YOU SITTING ON YOUR GREATNESS?

WE ALL HAVE A TESTIMONY!

We all have a testimony. I have come to realize is that without a test there is no testimony! Testimonies are faith stories. Our stories are our testimonies and they are not meant to be kept a secret. They are for us to share with others as a means to help them. It shows just how powerful our God is. All of us have a story which allows us to look at where we have come from and it gives us a different perspective so that we can see how grateful we should be for our lives and declaring God's grace and mercy in our lives. We all have stories that can be beneficial to others and remember with no test there will be no testimony.

Decide today that you will not sit on your greatness!

What is your testimony?

Do you believe in the power of testimonies?

What are your thoughts about sharing your testimonies?

What is God attempting to show you through your testimony?

WHY ARE YOU SITTING ON YOUR GREATNESS?

WE MUST ALWAYS BE PREPARED FOR OUR BLESSINGS!

The reason most people do not experience success is because they are not ready when success shows up. Someone once said, it is better to be ready and waiting for an opportunity than to have an opportunity and not be prepared for it! Unfortunately, it is usually the latter that is the case with most people. It is so important to stay ready at all times because God is always sending opportunities our way and we miss those opportunities because we are not ready for them when they appear. What is so heartbreaking is that people leave this earth without fulfilling their dreams. God never got to go into His bag of blessings for them. We have got to be ready for the blessings that God is constantly sending our way!

Decide today that you will not sit on your greatness!

Are you ready for your blessings?

Do you find yourself not being prepared when opportunities present themselves?

Are you ready for God to do some amazing things in your life?

Do you feel like you are not ready for your blessings?

What are you willing to sacrifice to prepare yourself for your greatness?

WHY ARE YOU SITTING ON YOUR GREATNESS?

WHAT ARE YOU DOING THAT IS PREVENTING YOUR GREATNESS FROM UNFOLDING?

Many things keep us from our greatness, especially a lack of a vision. The one thing that allows our power to unfold is when our vision motivates our actions. Waiting until you feel like working towards your greatness is not going to bring out your greatness. You will not always feel like doing the work, but you must keep going in spite of how you feel. That is when greatness comes in. Stop listening to the criticism of others no matter who they are. Keep your mind focused on your dreams, which will allow you to hear your thoughts and not the criticism of others. People who do not believe in your dreams will always attack them.

Stop making excuses for not doing what you need to do when you need to do it! "I'm not ready", "it's not the right time", "I'm not like everyone else", "I'm afraid of what others will think of me" - these are just a few of the excuses we feed ourselves, to avoid doing the work.

Procrastination: it keeps us from taking action because of fear of failure. Stay focused on your willingness to allow your greatness to unfold.

Decide today that you will not sit on your greatness!

Are you making excuses which ultimately stops your greatness from unfolding?

Do you find yourself procrastinating?

Do you allow the criticism of others to stop you?

Do you find yourself saying things like "you do not feel like it?"

What is keeping you from your greatness?

WHY ARE YOU SITTING ON YOUR GREATNESS?

WHAT ARE YOUR EXPECTATIONS ABOUT YOUR GREATNESS?

Here is what the dictionary has to say about expectations:

- A strong belief that something will happen or be the case in the future, "reality had not lived up to expectations."
- A belief that someone will or should achieve something, "high expectations for their future."

Great things happen when people have great expectations! The expectations that I have of my greatness is that it awaits me every day. God is putting great things before me to grab hold of and I am determined to take grasp of them all. I decided a long time ago that I would never wait around for others to give me their permission to be great. If we wait for others to tell that we are great, we will never experience the true greatness that God has for us. We do not have the time to wait on the permission of others, God has a lot for us to conquer in our lifetime and whatever we expect to happen in our lives will. The question is, who are you waiting on, yourself or the permission of others?

Decide today that you will not sit on your greatness!

Are you waiting for others to tell you that you are great?

What are your expectations for your life?

Do you believe in the great things God has in store for you?

Do you expect great things to happen in your life?

What are you confessing every day about your greatness?

WHY ARE YOU SITTING ON YOUR GREATNESS?

WHAT DOES GOD SAY ABOUT YOU?

"For I know the thoughts I think towards you, says the Lord, thoughts of peace and not evil, to give you a future and hope." Jeremiah 29:11.

"Your eyes saw my substance, being yet unformed. And in Your book, they all were written, the days fashioned for me, when as yet there were none of them, how precious also are Your thoughts to me O God! How great is the sum of them!" Psalm 139:16-17

"Are not two sparrows sold for a copper coin? And not one of them falls to the ground apart from your Father's will. But the very hairs on your head are all numbered. Do not fear therefore; you are of more value than many sparrows." Mathew10:29-31

"For we are His workmanship, created in Christ Jesus for good works, which God prepared beforehand that we should walk in them." Ephesians 2:10."

"I praise you because I am fearfully and wonderfully made; your works are wonderful, and I know that full well." Psalm 139:14

These scriptures tell us what God thinks about us. He loves us because He created us. To know who we are in Christ is key because He created us for greatness and nothing less!

Decide today that you will not sit on your greatness!

Do you believe you are made in greatness?

Do you trust God and what He has to say about you?

Do you believe God?

Who do you believe you are in Christ Jesus?

Who's artistry do you believe you are?

WHY ARE YOU SITTING ON YOUR GREATNESS?

WHAT EXCUSES ARE YOU SELLING YOUR GREATNESS?

It is time to do away with the excuses! We must stop telling ourselves these lies because we are not willing to do what is necessary to succeed. I was talking with one of my coaching clients and I asked her what was causing her to be in the same spot after 24 years. Her response was she did not know! I told her she did know she just had to figure it out. After asking her a series of questions she finally told me that she felt stuck. I gave her an exercise to do. I told her that once she did this exercise it would show her how to move to the next level.

The best way to handle being stuck is having someone who will listen to you and then walk you through the areas that you are unable to move past, instead of making up excuses to make yourself feel better about not moving forward. I read something by Dominic Soh that said, "I have no doubt you have your own set of dreams, goals, ambitions. You were born for greatness from the very start. But the distance between where you are right now and where you want to be can be measured by the number of excuses you make! The more excuses you make the bigger the distance. The fewer excuses you make the closer you are to your goals!"

Remember, excuses are the lies we feed ourselves to make us feel good about what we have not been willing to do. Let's turn our excuses into actions and make our goals a reality!

"Stop making excuses. Instead, excuse yourself and make something happen." Dominic Soh!

Decide today that you will not sit on your greatness!

What excuses are you feeding yourself?

Are you willing to stop making excuses?

Do you know why you keep making excuses?

Do you feel stuck?

What do you intend to do about it?

WHY ARE YOU SITTING ON YOUR GREATNESS?

WHAT LENS ARE YOU LOOKING THROUGH TO SEE YOUR GREATNESS?

Are you looking through a lens that is foggy or clear?

When you are looking through a foggy lens you are only able to see things negatively and as impossible. When you are looking through a clear lens, you can see all the possibilities as blessings from God! Foggy lenses could be the negative people who you have allowed to come into your life, people who have no vision or cannot see the possibilities because of their own foggy lens. They can make you doubt yourself and diminish your self-worth. The clear lenses help you see life from a better perspective. You see a life full of joy and peace. You feel confident and powerful. You are unapologetic about your life and your dreams and you do not feel like you need the permission of others to be great. Your ability to walk in your Greatness is clear and undeniable to the onlookers. When you have on a clear set of glasses, you see things the way God sees them.

Decide today that you will not sit on your greatness!

What are the possibilities you see for yourself ?

Are your lenses clear or foggy?

Are you unapologetic about your life and your dreams?

Is your greatness undeniable?

WHY ARE YOU SITTING ON YOUR GREATNESS?

WHERE YOU SEE DEFEAT, GOD SEES GREATNESS!

Did you know that where you see defeat, God sees greatness? The most important part about this journey we call "life" is we learn to see ourselves the way God sees us. When we spend too much time examining our lives, our problems, our success, and our failures it can become overwhelming. Through our point of view, we have to begin to see our greatness the way God sees it. Studying His word will tell you who you are in the eyes of God.

Write positive affirmations that will confirm who you are in Christ and read them daily to constantly remind yourself of who you are. Find friends who speak life into you when you need it and read books that will inspire you. Know that God always sees the best in us, we just need to see what He sees. Ephesians 1:18-19 says by having the eyes of your heart flooded with light so that you can know and understand the hope to which He has called you, and how rich is His glorious inheritance in the saints! Remember, where you see defeat, God sees greatness!

Decide today that you will not sit on your greatness!

Where do you see defeat in your life?

Do you see through your point of view or God's point of view?

Are willing to work on seeing yourself the way God sees you?

Do you realize God sees you as powerful and great?

Do realize that looking at things through the eyes of God will help you see your greatness?

WHY ARE YOU SITTING ON YOUR GREATNESS?

WHO IS IN YOUR CIRCLE OF INFLUENCE?

Relationships are an essential part of our lives. It is great to have relationships, but it is critical to have the right relationships. These are like-minded people who think positive and have big ambitions for their own lives. They are kind-hearted and compassionate. They do not make excuses for where they are in life and they take full ownership for their mistakes and are willing to move on and make the necessary changes. At some point you must decide to change your circle of influence, especially when you see that their decisions do not fit with yours. I can remember when I had to let go of a longtime friendship. It was hard but it was necessary. I felt like I was a better friend to her than she was to me. Sometimes we have to ask ourselves if this relationship has my best interest at heart and if the answer is no it is time to let that relationship go. Know that your circle of influence is the key!

Decide today that you will not sit on your greatness!

Do you have a positive circle of influence?

Are you happy with your circle of influence?

Is your circle of influence one that lifts you up or tears you down?

Do you feel the need to change your circle of influence?

Are you a people pleaser?

Do you find it hard to change your circle of influence even when you know it is not good?

WHY ARE YOU SITTING ON
YOUR GREATNESS?

CHAPTER 14

WHY ARE YOU SITTING ON YOUR GREATNESS?

YOU MUST BE WILLING TO FIGHT FOR YOUR GREATNESS!

I have come to realize is that most people are not willing to fight for their greatness. They will make all kinds of excuses for not fighting for what they want out of life. They will allow others to diminish their power and then play the victim just to have someone to blame for why they are not where they want to be in life. Your greatness is your responsibility. You must fight for what is yours, but in order to fight, you must have the fuel. It is essential to refuel your energy every day so you have the strength to fight for your greatness. You must pray, eat right and exercise your mind and body so that you can be healthy and on point. You must also watch out for those energy snatchers because they are out there, and they will take the energy that you need to fight for the life you want.

Here are some tips on how to fight for your greatness:
- Affirm that you are powerful every day.
- Create a Dream Book.
- Refuse to let others diminish your power.
- Only share with those that believe in you.
- Put yourself in the midst of like-minded people.
- Read books that inspire you.
- Talk with those that are going where you want to go.
- Delete all the negative people out of your circle.

Decide today that you will no longer sit on your greatness!

Are you willing to fight for your greatness?

Are you are sharing with the right people?

What do you do to keep yourself inspired?

Do you find it hard to delete negative people out of your life?

Are you allowing others to diminish your dreams?

WHY ARE YOU SITTING ON YOUR GREATNESS?

YOUR GREATNESS COMES FROM WITHIN!

"Greater is He that is in you than he that is in the world." 1 John 4:4

I love this scripture because it reminds me of the power that resides inside of me. There is no higher power than the power of Jesus Christ, which means that same power also resides within me. It helps me to realize that nothing is impossible for me and that I can do all things through Christ Jesus.

I want the light of Christ to shine so brightly that others will ask about the peace, joy, and love that radiates through me. When you are having a hard time, I want you to believe that the Greater One that is inside of you is so great that He can pull you out of any situation. Refuse to believe the lies the devil tells you and show him that you are a child of God and he will see that he has no power over you. God has given you the ability to defeat him. Remember that greater is He that is in you than he that is in the world!

Decide today that you will not sit on your greatness!

Do you realize that Christ can handle any situation in your life?

Do you believe the devil's lies or God's truth?

Do you realize that the Greater One is inside of you?

How bright is your light shining?

Do you realize all the possibilities you have with Christ?

WOMEN WHO CHOSE NOT TO
SIT ON THEIR GREATNESS!

CHAPTER 15

NORA SHARIFF-BORDEN

WHEN NORA STOPPED SITTING ON HER GREATNESS!

I was born in Boston, Massachusetts to Clyde and Audrey Morgan. My mother was 18 when she became pregnant with me and her father forced her to marry my father. She can remember wearing an old dress and stockings with runs in them on her wedding day - not a very beautiful day to remember. Shortly after they married, my father enlisted in the military and was sent overseas, leaving her to be a new mother alone. When he returned, he was a heroin addict and was physically abusive because of the drugs. She had 3 more daughters by him, and it was at this point she decided to leave.

Becoming a single mom raising four girls by herself was hard, but my mother had made up her mind that she wanted her daughters to have a better life than what she had.

Her mother had 6 children and when she was pregnant with her seventh child, which she did not want, she decided to have a "homemade abortion" and bled to death, leaving my grandfather with 6 children to raise on his own. He felt that he was not capable of doing so. He was offered help from my grandmother's side of the family but refused it and decided to take his children to New York instead. There he had a female friend, who my mother remembers was very mean to them - she hardly even fed them! My mother could remember being so hungry that she picked up an apple in the street to eat. She also tells the story about the time my Aunt Ruthie got on a train and rode from Harlem to Brooklyn to find my grandfather. She was only 4 at the time! My mother always finishes the story saying, "I do not know how she did it", but I do. I truly believe that it was God that lead her and held her hand!

Psalms 32:8 tells us that God will Instruct us and teach (show) us the way we should go. He will guide us with His eyes and watch over us! I believe that is what He did for that 4-year-old little girl, Ruth Miller. Aunt Ruthie found my grandfather and told him that his friend was mistreating them. He decided to take them back to Cambridge, Massachusetts to live with my grandmother's family.

Now I know why Psalms 32:8 means so much to me! My mother had a very rough life growing up. Caring for her siblings, then having to raise 4 children by herself, but she never gave up. She was determined to work hard to give us the best life that she knew how. We never knew that life was challenging and, looking back, I realize that she had a winner's mentality - the same mentality was gifted to me!

When I was just in the 6th grade, I remember a tall, white man with silver hair named Mr. Sullivan came to my classroom. He called my name and said he had to place me in a special needs classroom because I did not pass the school testing. Let me paint a picture of what a special needs classroom looked like back then in 1964. It was a classroom filled with the mentally challenged, deaf and blind. Since I was none of these things, you can only imagine what it did to my self-esteem. By the next year the Lord had a ram in the bush and his name was Mr. Nash! As long as I live, I will never forget the look in his eyes when he said to me, "you are smart, and you do not belong here. I am going to do everything in my power to help you get into a regular classroom," and he did just that! The following year I was placed into a regular 8th grade class. I realize now that was the voice of God speaking through Mr. Nash.

I graduated from the 8th grade and went on to high school. When I was in my second year of high school, not having my father in my life became evident and I started looking for love in all the wrong places. At the age of 16, I became pregnant with my first child, my son Lance. My mother was so hurt and upset because she did not want me to go through what she went through. It was at this time that I realized that I wanted and needed my dad in my life, but because of his pain, he was not available to me like I needed him to be.

Without judgment I would like to take a look into his life to explain why he was unable to be the father I once needed. You see, his father left him very early in his life, so he did not know what it was to be a father. I realize now that my dad was using drugs to soothe his own pain. My dad was very creative! He could create anything out of a piece of wood. Ultimately the drugs took his life. I realize my dad was just looking for love to fill a void, but he was looking for it in all the wrong places. The drugs became the substitute for the love he so desperately needed from his father and, like my dad, I needed that love from my father as well! Sadly, neither of us ever received that love. I love my dad and I miss him deeply. I wish he could have seen the great things that God had in store for him, but sadly he died taking his greatness to the grave with him.

Needless to say, I was lost! Still searching for myself and searching for love in all the wrong places, I made many mistakes. I can remember being homeless, with my 10-year-old son and a newborn baby daughter, Aminah. I remember we stayed at the Salvation Army for about 2 to 3 weeks. I decided to marry my daughter's father out of desperation, which was the worst decision I could have ever made. We should never make important decisions in desperate times! It was a horrible marriage and we became divorced after only 2 years of marriage. He was mentally abusive and that was the last thing I needed in my life. I remember on the day my divorce was final, I ran into the man that is now my husband today. He asked me out on a date which I replied, "no!" I knew that I needed time to heal and get to know myself after all I had been through. After about 2 years of his persistence, I finally said yes and the rest is history! We were married August 14th and this year we will have been together for 41 years and married for 31! I had finally found love.

I knew early on that I had an entrepreneurial spirit and decided to take a nail technician class so my best friend, Michelle, and I could open up a nail salon. We opened our salon right in the heart of Boston and it was beautiful. During that time I was also introduced to Mary Kay cosmetics, but was so focused on my nail salon I was not very interested. Sadly, the salon did not do too well and we ended up having to close our doors. It was then that I decided to operate my Mary Kay business full-time. My success came fast in Mary Kay, but I decided that I needed a change in my life. I moved from Boston to Durham, North Carolina where I had no family and no friends. I wanted to start fresh! I started my Mary Kay business all over again and laid another foundation in North Carolina. I must say, I was scared at first, but I did it anyway. I realized, despite all the challenges my mom had in her life, she never gave up. I thought about that often and allowed that to inspire me! She fought for a great life for herself and her children and I was going to do the same. Looking at my mom caused me to never give up on my dreams and to fight for what I wanted in life just like she did!

I was once sitting on my greatness, but I knew what I need to do to change that. I had to stop thinking about my dad and all his shortcomings and the pain of him not being there. I had to stop thinking about how hard my mom had it in life and look at the fact that she made it happen for herself and her family regardless of what she went through. I had to stop wishing that my parents raised me together like most of my friends that grew up with two parents in their household because that was not my story and I was allowing all of those things to rob me of my greatness! I decided to look at all the great qualities that my mom and dad did give to me.

Prior to coming into Mary Kay, I was a Muslim for eighteen years. Mary Kay reintroduced me to Christ, and I am grateful My Grandmother, Nora Dunn, was a Christian and introduced me to Christ when I was a little, but I got lost along the way.

I am proud to say today I am no longer sitting on my greatness but walking in it every day. My reason for writing this book was to show you how to face your failures in life and to take charge of your greatness.

I can remember when a friend of mine who was in the fashion industry asked me to write an article for a fashion magazine. I wrote the article and after reading it, the editor told me I could not write and that I would never be a successful writer. For so long I believed that lie, that is until the Lord breathed life into me and said, "write!" Imagine if I had allowed the voice of that editor to control my greatness! You would not be reading this book today. Now every time I think of her, I am inspired to write. Instead of allowing her words to stop me, they push me!

Congratulations on picking up this book and wanting to discover your God-given greatness. Congratulations on beginning your journey to your greatness!

"Don't be late on your assignment because you will miss your blessing!" I realized that God puts all thing in place for us to be great, but somehow, we get distracted. It is like the yellow brick road full of distractions. We have to stay focused on this journey to greatness. In Psalm 28:7, God tells us that His joy is our strength! I am so glad that I found the joy of the Lord to keep me strong on this journey because it has not been easy, but it is undoubtedly worth the fight!

Follow The Yellow Brick Road to Your Dreams!

VISION GOAL
Stay on the Yellow Brick Road!

Lack of Confidence

Love & Forgiveness

Positive Thinking

Bad Attitude

THESE ARE THE THINGS THAT WILL CAUSE YOU TO DETOUR OFF THE YELLOW BRICK ROAD!

Small Thinking

Positive People

Low Self-Esteem

Thinking Big Confidence

Negative People

Walking In Your Greatness

THESE ARE THE THINGS THAT WILL KEEP YOU ON THE YELLOW BRICK ROAD!

Faith Believe Trust

Fear

LAVONNDA BRANNON

FAITH IN THE MIDST OF TRAGEDY!

On August 18, 1988 my husband and I were blessed to deliver a healthy, six-pound baby boy, three weeks early. Daniel DeRay Brannon could not wait to be a part of this world. Daniel was our fourth child, and our third son. Daniel did not talk until he was 3 years old, although he could. When he did talk his words were full of wisdom. At the age of 5 he knew he wanted to go to the University of Alabama in Tuscaloosa. Daniel developed a love for music in elementary school, playing the cello and string bass and when he got to high school he started playing the quad drums. He received many scholarships for college to play in the band, however, Daniel no longer wanted to play in the band. His dream was to study Mechanical Engineering at The University of Alabama and that is exactly what he did. Daniel met many friends in college and was known as the dependable friend that would do anything for anyone. Many people looked up to him, especially his younger cousins.

On Friday, November 28, 2009, the day after Thanksgiving, Daniel was taking his cousins home. While sitting at a red light his car was struck from behind by a drunk driver. Little did I know that Daniel would die that night and that all of our lives would be changed forever!

People often ask how I dealt with the death of my son. It was not easy, but I found great peace knowing, not only was Daniel a great person but most importantly, he was saved, and had a great relationship with God. Daniel had also made the decision to become an organ donor and was able to give 5 people a better quality of life.

The Bible tells us in John 16:33 in this life we will have troubles, but God will give us a peace that surpasses all understanding. That is exactly what He has done for me.

In the months following Daniel's death I found myself praying even more for the people around me. One thing that really moved me was on the Sunday after Daniel died 82 kids gave their lives to Christ. I found myself in that moment experiencing that peace that God was talking about in John 16:33.

Almost 12 months later, I was faced with having to deal with true forgiveness when at the court hearing for the 31-year-old male that made a terrible decision to drive while under the influence of alcohol that night. I had to put myself in this young man's shoes and realize that everyone makes mistakes. I realized he did not intentionally seek out to kill my son. I have made mistakes in my life and God has forgiven me, so therefore I must forgive others.

Each day I make a choice to live my life like Christ with a loving heart. I am so very thankful for the 21 years that God allowed me to spend with my son Daniel and I pray that he continues to live through me every day.

JOANNE BARNES

FROM SOUL KNOWING TO SPIRIT LEARNING

I am a firm believer that all of us are here on a spiritual journey with a calling on our life that has a divine plan and a divine purpose. It is only now that I can say with all certainty that my soul always knew this truth, but my life experiences brought me to this awareness.

As a young girl growing up in the countryside of Virginia, church and school were the only activities that made our lives. My life was wrapped up in going to church every Sunday and oftentimes, prayer meetings in the middle of the week. Entertainment beyond those walls were not permitted. Our family was the builders of our small town Baptist church.

Added to this was the fact that integration found its way to our town. In third grade three "colored kids" from every grade level were chosen from the all black school to be bused to all white schools to see how integration would work. My first cousin, my twin sister and myself were the chosen ones. This experience truly shaped who I would become. For the sake of this writing it will suffice to say that my journey was marked with a lot of emotion and hard work to be the best at everything, especially academically as it was "required." Graduating from high school in 1971, college was not much of a focus for our family. None of my immediate family had succeeded at that endeavor however, my twin sister and I decided we would try, especially since I had a burning desire to become a teacher since I was 5. After all, pretending to teach all of the neighborhood kids growing up was how we entertained ourselves. How would this ever be possible without the necessary credentials required for higher learning? We accomplished that lofty endeavor and would both go on to be highly successful in our chosen fields. Life set in and 2 years after college I would suffer an emotional breakdown that marked the beginning of a very broken life.

Next would come marriage and by the age of 25 I was now clinically depressed with 3 children, a husband, a home with 2 cars in the driveway and a "good job" working in corporate America. My high school sweetheart and I had managed to create what appeared to be the perfect life. That lasted all of 8 years and now the downward spiral was apparent.

Twenty years in the legal field felt like a trap and again my children would watch their mom go through an even deeper depression which had me questioning whether this life was even worth it. Many times, attempting to escape it all. Religion was still a major part of who I was - the searching for truth at its best. I would soon discover many great teachers along my journey, each of them always showing up at exactly the right time. One of those teachers was called pain, which was always a great teacher as long as you learned the lessons it will lovingly attempt to provide.

An answer would come at the age of 38, an opportunity to own my own business. I would spend the next 28 years discovering my spirituality and myself. When I walked away from the corporate world from many adventurous and high level places everyone thought that I had really lost my mind "this time", especially the people who meant the most to me, my family. This is where my soul knew it was time to test my faith and go for something that might just quench the burning desire to fulfill my calling to teach. I learned there is power in decision when you stand in your decision without wavering. Perhaps this is why we are taught biblically that an indecisive man can expect nothing at all. Following this calling on my life and living the fulfillment of that God-given assignment would earn me an honorary title of Emeritus (an honorary title for a person retired from professional life holding the ranking of the last office held).

The journey from being broken in so many places to becoming a master mender and now teacher was challenging but at every step of the way I would discover, notice and express gratitude for the assistance of a master teacher, the Holy Spirit. He taught me in quiet times. In the middle of the night I would often be awakened to study as messages were imprinted in my mind. There were many spiritual hands along the way.

What I know for sure is that God was always guiding me, even when I chose not to listen. It did not matter the challenge! What I discovered was myself and my spiritual connection. This is a connection each person always has as long as we have breath in our body and choose to be open to guidance. Life is all about choices.

It still intrigues me as I am reminded daily of His presence in my life. Always directing, always teaching and reminding me that it is in Him that I "move and breath and have Life." My teaching today has been elevated beyond my wildest imagination because I chose to be a student of life with a 28 year apprenticeship! I loved working for myself where no paycheck was ever guaranteed.

Find what you love, honor that God-given desire and allow God to unfold it! Surrender and watch as He creates a panoramic view of a life that you will look back on with awe and will bear your name.

DR. CYNTHIA L. HALE

I HAD NO INTENTIONS ON BEING A PREACHER!

My parents named me Cynthia, which means "bringer of light." My ministry began as the resident "student pastor" on my high school campus, leading a Bible study before school and counseling students when they were in trouble or in pain. I had never seen or heard of a woman in ministry, so I would never say that I was in ministry or admit that I would ever be, even though the folks in my church and the community said otherwise. I ignored them, because I had no intention of being a preacher.

It was during my senior year of high school that the opposition to my ministry began. I lead a young man named Richard to Christ. After Richard got a few Bible verses under his belt, he announced to the group that I would no longer be permitted to teach Bible study. He based his decision on I Timothy 2:11-12, where Paul says, *"a woman should learn in quietness and full submission. I do not permit a woman to teach or to have authority over a man; she must be silent."*

I quickly reminded him that I was not a woman yet and he was not a man.

Nevertheless, I stepped down and became Richard's student, even though I was the one who had been studying the Bible for about eight years and him only about eight weeks. Little did I realize that all of this was preparing me for many future confrontations with men and women too, who did not believe that women should preach.

After high school, I attended Hollins College where I majored in music. The chaplain, Alvord Beardslee, told me that I had the gifts and graces for ministry. I paid him no attention, but was very interested in religion, so I became active in the chapel program while pursuing a degree in music education.

Hollins was where I grew up, where I faced the real world of racism and discovered that I had to be better than the best as an African American woman. It was at Hollins that I discovered that I needed to become academically and intellectually strong and I did. It was at Hollins that I came into my own and discovered the power of being a gifted African American woman who believed in her God and herself.

I learned that lesson as I struggled with low self-esteem and insecurity that caused me to question my self-worth at every turn. I had never felt so unsure of myself before. It was then that God spoke profoundly to me through Psalm 139, helping me to affirm that I am fearfully and wonderfully made in God's image and likeness.

During my sophomore year Alvord Beardslee announced that he was going on sabbatical. A committee was established, of which I was a part, to choose his replacement. When a woman's name was suggested, I was vehemently opposed to it, saying no woman will ever preach to me. A year later, I received my call in an undeniable way.

I went to Seminary at Duke and fell in love with ministry. I was surrounded by some of the most dynamic men and women who had a heart for God and a heart for God's people. In that place, we studied and prayed, dialogued and sharpened one another for the task of ministry. At Duke, I settled once and for all the question of whether or not I was called to preach. Not all of the men believed that I had been called to preach and told me so on a regular basis. I must admit, the constant put down and questions caused me to doubt the call, but I would not give up.

God sent sweet confirmations, through people like Gardner C. Taylor who told me that if God called me to preach, not to worry about what others think and say, God never wastes His material. Those words helped me understand that I did not need to fight or try to defend my call. I just needed to know that God had called me and would use me. My gifts would make room for me and they did.

One of my classmates invited me to preach at the Federal Men's Prison in Butner, North Carolina. The day that I went to the prison, the Head Chaplain, a Catholic Priest, asked if I would take the position of protestant chaplain. I agreed and worked there for 18 months. When I graduated from seminary, the Head Chaplain resigned, and I was given his position, making me the first female to serve as chaplain in an all-male federal prison.

Being a female in an all-male prison was quite an experience. The inmates loved me, but the staff fought me in every way. Why was I as a woman serving in an all-male prison? They were convinced that I was there looking for a man. There were times I wanted to give up and go home, but God would not let me. I wanted to sit down on my greatness, but God gave me the strength to stand in the midst of fierce opposition.

What I sought to do was to bring a sense of balance and normalcy in a place where dysfunctionality and human frailty were so evident. I learned in that prison about loving unconditionally, treating all persons with dignity and respect, being present with persons in their lowest and weakest hour, knowing that I represent God. I love to say that I learned how to be a pastor in prison.

I served in the prison for five years, before being reassigned to the Federal Law Enforcement Center in Brunswick, Georgia as a staff instructor. The intention of the Prison Administration was to transition me into an Associate Warden position because of my strong gifts in administration, but I was clear that I was called to ministry.

Shortly thereafter, the Christian Church's soon-to-be-elected General Minister and President called to ask if I would consider being one of his deputies.

My position would include being the General Secretary of the National Convocation, the Black Fellowship of our church. There was a merger agreement that said that the leaders of the National convocation were to be consulted as to who they wanted to see in that position.

Without consulting them, Dr. Humbert offered me the position. Not a good move because at the General Assembly where he was to be elected and his deputies confirmed, the brothers and sisters protested my appointment, saying I was not qualified to lead them. They said I was too young, that I had never served as a Pastor, so how could I serve Pastors. They even went on to say in an article in the Des Moines paper that I could not pastor a Black Church. They felt I did not have what it would take.

They never said that they could not accept my nomination because I was a woman, but many believe that was the real issue, despite the fact that I had just completed a term as the youngest persons and first female to serve as President of the National Convocation.

Needless, to say this was the most painful and humiliating experience that I have ever had. I often refer to that as my Calvary experience. I felt like my colleagues had crucified me. That experience taught me the reality of church politics, racism, and sexism. I know that my brothers and sisters meant me no personal harm - they felt violated by the system and I felt violated, too.

Time healed my hurt and also helped me to see that God does indeed "work together in all things for the good of those who love him and are called according to his good pleasure." During the time that I was being interviewed by the General Office, I also received a call to become a Pastor Developer of a new church in Atlanta. In all honesty, that was not nearly as exciting to me as the Deputy General Ministry position, but I was not looking at it from God's perspective. God sees the end from the beginning and had awesome plans for me in Georgia. I was dealing with what appeared to be the most attractive and prosperous at the moment.

Starting a church was not exactly what I had in mind. I just knew that God would give me a ready-made situation. What God gave me was an opportunity to develop a ministry that had my design and His on it. So, after Calvary came the resurrection and the ascension. I did rise again.

The woman that they said could not pastor a Black Church became the founding pastor of the Ray of Hope Christian Church in January 1986. It was the best thing I have ever done. The church grew from four members to 8,000, from four ministries to 40, through which we are fulfilling our vision, "to impact and transform the present world into the Kingdom of God!"

Dr. Cynthia L. Hale
Senior Pastor
Ray of Hope Christian Church
Decatur, Georgia

BRIDGET SHAW

I CHOSE TO TRUST JESUS!

It was an unusually hot August. My daughter, Kayla and I had gone to Dallas for a business trip. We got home, flipped our suitcases and met the boys for family vacation in Myrtle Beach, South Carolina. We were there for seven days and returned home at 2 am on Saturday morning. We had so much to get done in the next 24 hours!

Ken left home at 8:30 am for meetings. I dropped Josh off for a fresh haircut. School was starting on Monday. Kayla was at home getting her belongings together. She was moving into a new apartment and starting her senior year at USC. I was headed to the studio for makeovers. Everyone had something important to do.

Ken picked Josh up and they went to tell Kayla goodbye because they would be at church when she and I left for the move in. I was managing it all over the phone while making my way back to our home of 13 years. I called Kayla to ask if she would consider staying one more night. She said, "no." Through all of the hustle, none of us realized our world would change forever.

Kayla called me frantically. "Mom! The house is burning down!" I was less than a mile from home. I quickly called Ken and asked him where he was. He had just arrived at the church. I explained what was happening and told him to meet me at home immediately.

As I drove into my neighborhood police cars and fire engines were everywhere. The main road was blocked off, but I drove as far as I could and ran bare foot the rest of the way until I could see my only daughter. She was standing in my neighbor's yard in her pajamas with an officer. I saw the blaze but it was not my focus. I remember asking Kayla if she was ok and where our pets were.

I remember turning, almost in slow motion, as I to a look at what had betrayed me. In that moment the Holy Spirit captured my thoughts and whispered, "it is just stuff." Before a tear could drop, I was reminded of life, salvation and the word! God had promised me when I accepted Jesus as my Lord and Savior that He would never leave me nor forsake me.

Within minutes, people from all over the world came to assist. They visited, sent money and gift cards, brought clothes and food. Most importantly, they loved us which made us never feel alone. When the Red Cross arrived the representative said she had never seen such an outpouring of love and protection.

Physically we were fine - the emotions of it were yet to come. My Joshua lost the only home he had ever known and began displaying anger. Kayla soon left for college dealing with emotions she could not articulate. Ken and I were overwhelmed with the details of building a new home while taking the one of thee biggest promotion of a lifetime - we were finishing a National Area.

After the fire, a dear friend sent me a Bible and a devotional, *Jesus Calling*. These tools were such a gift because the fire was the first attack. Just a few weeks after came the mammoth attack. I lost friends that I considered to be family. *Jesus Calling* was what I needed at this time in my life. I committed to studying and journaling every morning. It started with tears, hurt and anger. I prayed and asked for forgiveness for my part in the situation and for the ability to forgive them. Emotionally, every morning I made a decision that I would deal with the hurt and the pain. God's word gave me the energy to get through my day.

I had to decide to trust Jesus! I did not care what it looked like. I knew if He could get my only daughter and my fur babies out of a burning home with no injuries, He could finish a National Area and restore relationships! It was a daily process. The first words I wrote for months on my journal were, "I TRUST JESUS!" It did not always seem possible but I knew I could trust Jesus. He sent the people I needed, the resources I needed, and the peace I needed. All I had to do was trust Him and work as if it were already done!

Everything has been restored tenfold! We have a beautiful family home and are all healthy and whole. In addition, I am A National Sales Director of the Dream Big Area!

CATERINA HARRIS EARL

MY DAD, MY BEST FRIEND!

In one moment your whole life can change and I do not think you are ever fully prepared for it. It is in that moment that everything you know, the bricks of your life that have been laid brick by brick over the years to build your strong and solid foundation, strengthen you and help you to stand tall. I know that I was privileged to have an amazing dad. A strong relationship that not everyone has with their father, a father who was my #1 cheerleader, my best advisor, my best friend, and even my business partner.

"I prayed for a man and the Lord sent me my daddy." I said jokingly in my 30's. For over 10 years we built a great life together and in addition to being the best dad who continued to be stern and loving at the same time, he also played a major role in helping me to become a successful entrepreneur. You name it, he would do it. He helped with all things technical, helped me produce life-changing events and kept things moving on the home front to allow me to travel the world as he once had in his former years as an aircraft engineer. Then one moment it happened! I woke up on a bright, early Sunday morning talking about him and within three hours found out he slipped into eternity during the night. Although I had a strong faith, nothing prepared me to say goodbye like this. No more encouraging talks, no more midnight movies, no more laughter, no more tears of joy as I observed his grin as he looked at me. There would only be memories.

In this process of grieving and making sense of it all, I was so grateful for the bricks laid in my life. Many of them laid by my father and my amazing mother. Many more laid by the "village" that raised me and then even more from the amazing girlfriends that have encouraged me in my adult life. Bricks that helped me to be strong and of good courage. It is one thing to be a hearer of God's word and an entirely different thing to be a doer of His word.

"Fear not, for I am with you; be not dismayed, for I am your God. I will strengthen you, yes, I will help you, I will uphold you with My righteous right hand" (Isaiah 41:10). God promised to be with me and get me through the most intense times of disappointment and loneliness.

I learned to let the tears flow, but keep it moving. Not just moving to be busy but moving to press toward the next level in life. God knows in advance and He prepares us along the way. I look back to see how even though I did not feel as if I was prepared, God had been preparing me all along. I can see His hand on it all. He always is a very present help in time of need.

The heartache of missing dad will never disappear, but the mantle has been passed and I accepted it. The best and only way to truly celebrate the life of someone who lived so well is to live well! As I entered the newest chapter of my life, it gave me an opportunity to redefine whom I was and what I was called to do. I am called to empower others to find their passion and live their dreams. This is a part of the process to prepare me for those I am called to lead. I have often been more empowered by watching how someone triumphs in adversity than how they celebrate during victories. What a testimony that I now have. Almost weekly, I have the opportunity to encourage others who endure huge and unexpected loss and while I cannot say, "I know how you feel" because I do not, I can tell them with all sincerity, "you will be stronger than ever because of it."

You are not made to break, you are stronger than you think. I learned to be broken before God as He helps me to be whole. I did not lose my father. I did not lose a part of me. I actually found out more of who I was and what I was capable of. I can look at every man, woman, and child and assure them they are stronger than they think.

PAMELA SHAW

MY LIFE WAS ON COURSE UNTIL...

My life was "on course"- playing out as beautifully as I had optimistically imagined it would. An adoring and hard-working husband, a bright and engaging 10-year-old son, a thriving business at the top of my game, living close to my parents and siblings - all interrupted one day by a speech slur.

Jerry, age 39, a former University of Florida football player and tri-athlete had always been to his friends "superman," and to me was a rock, my protector, my partner in every way. He was a pillar of physicality and strength. This growing speech slur sent us on a journey for answers to many medical professionals, turning first to traditional neurology and related practitioners only to quickly run to a holistic world of possible cures for the unexplained. Four months into advancing symptoms, a diagnosis - ALS. The year that followed was heart breaking at best. We continued to search for naturopathic cures, something to slow it down. As each function of his physical life faded before our eyes, we had a choice to make. Would I stand on the faith I had professed for a lifetime? Would he keep the faith, even though he faced life's ultimate challenge – disease in one's own physical body. How would we parent? What would this mean for our son, for our business, for me? Do I continue to work? What is in front of us? How long does he have? Do we have? There were so many unknowns.

It is "easy" as a believer to keep the faith when your blessings overflow - when the scriptures that seem to reward discipline and obedience are manifesting in your life. I would call that "baby" Christian understanding. God is blessing me because of my great love for Him, because I desire to please Him in all I do and say and because I am obedient in my private life and honor His word through daily disciplines and prayer, Bible Study, church, etc. Not in a legalistic way. In true love and devotion. But what happens to faith when bad things happen to good people? A choice will be made.

During the years of his struggle through ALS to death, I never asked "why". Keenly aware of a hurting world, I knew we had been blessed. We had a fairy tale love story, solid marriage, were world travelers, amazing opportunities, a beautiful son, daily moments full of joy and extraordinary experiences some will never know. But then there was the stark reality. I am a young widow and single parent to now 12-year old Thomas who was entering puberty. I now have to hire eight virtual assistants to do what Jerry did in our office, while I figure out how to grieve. My life was public, sort of a fishbowl. My deep desire to be authentic, raw, honest and true to my faith in Christ was strong and real. But what does that look like with the magnitude of this loss none of which was in my picture, my dreams, my prayers, my vision board, my affirmations? Since "why" was not my question, I dug in deep for "what." What do I do now? What do you do when life interrupts?

Initially, I made simple day-to-day decisions. I kept things as normal for my son as I could - school, sports and a family schedule was something that made sense. My parents were visible and available. But the lonely nights. My empty bed. The emails I would start to him before the reality of his death would stop my typing. The questions I needed to run past him. I battled depression, foreign to me in the context of my life. This lingered. I could go on and on, but I knew I had to park on the ultimate truth.

Each of our days are numbered. Psalm 90:12 "Teach us to make the most of our time so that we may grow in wisdom." I wanted to live, to be healthy, to serve, influence, make a difference - to fulfill God's calling on my life. Life would never be the same, but I would say "yes Lord" to His plan. It would become my "best" yes all over again. His ways are not our ways; His thoughts are not our thoughts. But His promise to never leave or forsake us is solid and I leaned in. Instead of "why us", "why not us?" If I believed in an omniscient God, that a destiny for each of us includes an eternal life, and if I was choosing to stand on this, then I would also have to live it.

The next chapter opened up another uninvited, unexpected journey with my son - that of addiction. Although I recognized the enemy's interest in the destruction of our lives, it did not make the navigation easier. From counseling to rehabs to male mentors who tried to step in, this season of life as I had imagined it also crumbled. Instead of college, involvements, academic success and graduation, the many starts/stops/intervention/support/start-overs were centered more around recovery than acceleration. His amazing story is still being written, but who I continue to become in the process of the unplanned, uninvited, unexpected is the journey through faith - to faithfully stay in my lane and to believe in what I know God has intended for good.

During my earliest and deepest grieving, I found a world class counselor. She and her husband are on video for most "Grief Share" classes in church. She guided me well and with wisdom and coached me how to define and create "new normal." As I grieved all over again the unexpected journey of my son, I had to learn what it means to "capture every thought." I am still learning and still practicing that discipline. Romans 12:2 "Do not be conformed to this world, but be transformed by the renewing of your mind…" I know that as my thinking goes, so goes my life. I want to live in love, gratitude, joy, peace, patience, kindness, confidence and to stand in the fullness of God's calling. I choose life!

Through my life journey I have learned that God will bring to you (and me) what and who we need just when we need it. He is always on time, never late, rarely early. It is a close faith walk. Just speaking the name "Jesus" in the middle of a negative or debilitating thought brings peace and love. A simple "I trust you Lord" brings a rogue thought captive. As others looked on to my choices to see if I would show up, hide, cave, cower, stick to my faith story or change it, I knew my testimony was at risk. Although I have made many mistakes, failed many times, fallen short often, my faith has not faltered. I stand on solid rock and God has proven faithful. Yes, I have cried out in many emotions, but

I know the one true God is still on the throne. It is not "my will" but His. That He who began a good work in me will be faithful to complete it. When trials come, and they will, my choice to trust in God's goodness, faithfulness, love and provision comes down to just that - a choice.

PATRICE SMITH

MY TRUST IN THE LORD

"Trust in the Lord with all thine heart; and lean not unto thine own understanding. In all thy ways acknowledge him, and he shall direct thy paths." (Proverbs 3:5-6)

The prevailing question for every believer is, do we have the faith to trust God like we should? Can we trust Him even when we cannot trace Him? Can we trust Him through the trying times of our faith? Can He trust us to hold on to Him when we cannot see clearly?

These questions have looked me square in my face many times. None quite as piercingly as when, after giving birth to our twins, I received a letter in the mail stating that something irregular was detected in baby A's blood work and that I needed to return with her for further evaluation. Upon running subsequent tests we, as young, brand new parents were told that our precious baby girl had Sickle Cell Anemia! What happened? We prayed. We believed. We confessed. Yet, this was the report that was given to us. We were confused, hurt and afraid. "God! Where are You?? How and why?" In that pivotal moment I had to decide, "Lord I have no other choice but to trust You!"

Our journey with the Lord and this report concerning our daughter, and four years later our youngest son, has been one filled with many tears, sleepless nights, painful hospital stays, fears every time the phone rang with a call from the school and many questions. Yet in times when I felt slayed I had to say, "yet will I trust You." Through the most trying times when giving up would have been easy, when making excuses for why they could not and even why I could not achieve.

God kept bringing us through, He kept healing, He kept restoring and our faith kept increasing as we stood on His word that they would be healed regardless of what it looked like and regardless of man's report. We learned to work the word, decree the word to call those things that be not as though they were!

That was 24 years ago and God's faithfulness reigns! I was able to build a successful business with Mary Kay Cosmetics from the beginning level all the way to the top leadership position in the company as a National Sales Director. Our daughter has matriculated through school to obtain degrees from Spelman College and Wake Forest University. She is now employed in her dream job as a Business Analyst in Dallas, Texas. My son is now 20 years old and is a junior in Public Relations at Florida A&M University. Both are doing well and walking in their healing and giving back! As a result of their journey they co-founded SICK OF IT - a foundation that gives support, mentors and educates Sickle Cell Warriors and their families.

I am so grateful God trusted us with this assignment to bless many from our journey. We learned to take Him at His word and conquer life rather than life conquering us!

DR. GLORIA MAYFIELD BANKS

I FOUND SUCCESS IN THE MIDST OF DYSLEXIA!

When I was in the 7th grade, I was diagnosed with Dyslexia. My teacher called my mother with concern after I had to do a book report, and I cut up my textbook because I found it hard to do the research. My book report had given her some clues that suggested I had some issues and she suggested that they test me.

My parents found my diagnosis difficult at first because they were both educators. They could not figure out how they missed it! My mom would stay up with me night after night to help me with my school work, but I still could not get it.

The only way I could seem to understand was when I memorized the information and it is the same way today. I could not spell things out loud unless I memorized them and I had a hard time understanding math equations. But my parents were always behind us 100% and committed to solving problems while making sure my confidence stayed active and in tack. My parent became determined to help me overcome this issue!

Oddly enough my diagnosis did not seem to effect me socially. I loved people and was the head of my cheerleading team. I knew early on how to rally others to success because it was fun, and I loved it!

During testing, I needed extra time and would miss school when I knew we had a test because I was afraid I would not finish in the time that was given to me. I would stare at the paper and because I could not read it quickly enough, I would shut down which caused me a great deal of stress.

I had to take on a lot of extra courses in school and needed a tutor. I had a teacher who took additional interest in me. She was my business teacher in high school. She and my mother became good friends because they spent so much time guiding me through high school.

My high school schedule was crazy. In order to succeed, I would ride to school an hour early in the morning. Then finish school and take a bus another hour to Wayne State University for an individual business class. I thought I wanted to be a Court Recorder. The problem with that was I could type what I saw, but I could not spell on my own. Needless to say, my educational journey was very challenging.

I loved going to church and I became very active in my church. I would read almost every Sunday from the Bible. God cleared the way for me to read out loud at church events which I loved to do!

During my time at Harvard, I had a good friend name Juliana who would help me with studying and testing. She would read aloud to me which helped me with my study habits. I also believed it was my constant mind shift and a positive attitude which kept me going. I pushed through, no matter what was in front of me. I learned the gift of gab, which increased my personality and I used it to excel at school and work.

I value the kindness of the teachers who took the extra time to care for me. It was tough to reveal to them my weakness, but when I did, I found they wanted to help me, and the fear was all in my mind.

One of my biggest obstacles was pulling myself out of domestic violence. It was very hard, and it took a long time. I was able to create a vision of what my life might be like if I could find my way out instead of fighting to save a marriage that was detrimental to me and my children!

I believe my strength in overcoming all life obstacles has been my emotional management. When I stop thinking and feeling sorry for myself I go onto the next situation I had to handle. I refuse to let others experience my pain by talking about it all the time and thinking it was ok for them to listen to my issues. Telling the story over and over only keeps the story alive. I decided to push forward no matter what I was going through.

It was not easy, nor did I expect it to be. I just had to keep one foot in front of the other, increase my income, get a great lawyer, stay in the circle of the right people, and take care of my children no matter what it took.

I believe my self-esteem could have been crushed because of all the words and deeds done to me by my ex-husband, but my parents did an exceptional job building me and my self-esteem up so no one person or one situation could take it down.

Dyslexia, it is not something you overcome. It is a state of reality like a leg that is to short or four fingers instead of five. I have learned not to let dyslexia or any obstacle determine the outcome of my life. I am utterly transparent with others - I can shout "I am dyslexic" many times when I am speaking and I refuse to let it bother me!

"Reveal where you might be weak so others who are strong in those areas can show up for you and receive you with open arms."

CHERYL MORGAN WILSON

THE LOVE OF A SON

One of the most devastating calls a mother could ever receive is your child is dead. Saturday, April 8, 2017, I was preparing my church for a small wedding. It was a beautiful day the sun was shining the birds were singing and not a drop of rain in sight, which was a dream come true for the bride. We had prepared the wedding decorations the night before and my responsibility was to decorate the church the morning of the wedding. I was alone at the church listening to one of my favorite songs "I am a friend of God, He calls me friend" I could hardly wait for Saturday to come, to see the wedding procession, the groom and minister set in place, and then everything stops as the bride in all her glory marches down the aisle to become one with her future husband. I love wedding planning and making others feel special.

Suddenly the music stopped and my phone rang. I proceeded to answer the phone and I will never forget the frantic voice at the other end of the call. I could hardly understand what she was saying through her tears and screams. I knew at that point something was drastically wrong. I remember asking her to calm down and tell me what she was saying. She then proceeded to say, "there was a tragedy at work and I think your son is dead." I asked her to call me back when she was certain. This is when I knew I had to have reckless faith to respond to this horrific situation. I shouted to the enemy this is war you will not destroy this wedding or me, and I proceeded to tell God I trusted you, and you are in control.

I had realized a long time ago that my son did not belong to me but to Him. I proceeded to worship God and dance and dance and dance I then fell to my knees telling God, "I trust you, I trust you, I trust you. He is yours." I said a prayer and I continued to decorate the church.

Moments later I received a call from one of my minister friends in Boston, Massachusetts who told me the news of my son was on the Internet. I then hung up and called my sisters, family and friends to tell of the tragic news - my son had killed himself and others.

I then went home showered and came back to the wedding without telling anyone what was happening. I was waiting for the confirmed call from the Miami police department. I made a statement to the devil that he would not destroy this wedding or me. I knew at that point that God had me in the palm of His hands, because I could see His foot prints in the sand of my heart. I feel His peace that surpass all understanding, and His eyes are watching me.

There was no way I could have sustained this tragedy of my only child without the power of God. My son was about to celebrate his 34th birthday in August and had his whole life a head of him. He was an inspiration to many. He was a protector and a good son.

I realize through all of my heartache and pain, death is a door we all have to enter into. We do not know the day, the time or the how. I chose not to sit on my greatness the moment I got the news. We must realize that the Greater one is inside us, and that He is everything we need. Because He lives in us we can face tomorrow. Forthcoming is my new book *Reckless Faith through Obedience, Authenticity, and Generosity.*

SABRINA GOODWIN MONDAY

THE PUREST FORM OF LOVE

I lost my best friend, December 8, 2015. She was 78. There was no diagnosis of exactly what my mom passed away from, but she was hospitalized with health issues and never returned home. That was the saddest day of my life. I remember leaving the hospital, going to her home, walking in those doors, and the house felt hollow. Her physical presence was greatly missed immediately. I slept in her bed that night. Still wanting to be as close to her as possible. I remember the smell of her bed sheets, fragrant like her, they comforted me.

My mom was the most positive influencer in my life. She was an amazing woman, always uplifting, and always looking for the good in everybody and all situations. In her last days, barely able to talk, with little strength she hugged me and uttered, "I'm so proud of you and your beautiful family." The very last words, that I heard her speak, were to pastor Kim, who had come to offer prayer in her last days, barely opening her eyes, she glanced up and said "you look so pretty." Yep, with her last words, she was lifting somebody up.

My mother was my greatest cheerleader. I was always amazed how she maintained such a positive attitude raising 4 children, when life was not always easy. I understand now she chose to live in peace, harmony and happiness. My mom's first name was Alquita, the name as unique as she, her middle name Joy, which certainly spoke to the emotion she blessed us all with.

As I look back on my childhood, it was not ever "can we do it", it was always "when will we do it?" I was privileged to grow up with an encouraging, supportive mother, who loved us unconditionally. I am grateful.

I was talking to a friend, just yesterday, we were talking about my mom, and she expressed how blessed we were, to be raised with such positivity. In tears and with great sadness, my friend went on to share her relationship with her mom was totally different, filled with animosity, judgment and non-belief. She said she tried for years to mend and build the relationship, and finally 4 years ago, decided to stop trying. They have not spoken since. This is hard for me to imagine. Your mother, her daughter. The conversation made me sad, prayerful and thankful.

My mother was the real deal. I grew up respecting her charm, grace, dignity in which she lived. She was clear in her communication. We knew she meant business. She was as loving and loyal as they come, just do not cross her. Alquita Joy affectionately better know as "Queet" to family and friends was the gatherer. She was the crowd pleaser. Everybody always ended up at her home. Maybe just maybe, because you could always find good eats at Queet's. She was famous for her homemade rolls, macaroni and cheese and tacos. She never cooked just enough for our family, because there was always company at 762 N. Denver. My mom loved cooking; she was forever stirring something in that black cast iron skillet. She was never in a hurry when she cooked; I think that is why it always tasted so good. The kitchen was where we would have the best conversations; she sure knew how to turn a house into a home.

As I entered young adulthood, it was so much fun and rewarding sharing secrets, recipes, and getting relationship/career advice from my mom. She was the most incredible listener. She was never quick to speak on an issue, but when she did, it was time to listen, very wise in her counsel. My mother was an avid reader, very intelligent, witty, and always leaving you in the conversation with the confidence that you could and would make the best decisions for your life.

During grad school, while living in Boston, I could not wait for my mom to visit me on the east coast. We loved to travel to NYC and Martha's Vineyard. My mother and I were a lot alike. She was snazzy and jazzy, we loved to shop for designer outfits and shoes together. She was always the life of the party and had a great sense of style. Yep, I get it from my mama.

My mother was diagnosed with cancer in 2008. She fought it like a champ. Never complained, always looking on the bright side of things. Of course, we wanted her to get the best care, and Christmas 2010 we found ourselves in MD Anderson hospital in Houston, TX, I remembered saying, "Mom when you get up and out of here, we will celebrate big time this time next year." Mom's rare cancer surgery of the lower-intestine went well, she recovered nicely, and that next year, we spent Christmas 2011 on the Amalfi Coast in Italy, visiting my oldest daughter Sydnee, who had just graduated from high school and was studying abroad. It was just myself, my older brother Greg, and my younger sister Regina and our mom! I am so glad we took the time to create wonderful memories of a lifetime. We never had laughed so hard. Laughter is good for the soul, my family loves to laugh, it was a constant in our childhood home in Tulsa, Oklahoma.

As I get older, so many say, I am looking more like my mom, and I sound like her too. That makes me feel good all over. I have always said, if I could be 1/3 of the mother to my children, that my mom was to me, they would have something great. My mom had the uncanny ability to make all 4 of her children believe they were her favorite. My oldest brother Eric; preceded her in death as he was tragically killed in a car accident at the age of 31. Watching mother bury her first born and walk though that time in life with such strong faith, never bitter, always striving to become better taught me much. To this day, I find myself regularly thinking and saying what would Queet do in this situation, and a calm resolve comes over me.

She was a great daughter, sister, wife, mother, aunt, cousin, grandmother and friend. My children adored Grandma Queet; she loved sports and would talk trash with the best of them.

She has left a great legacy of life lessons, love and laughter. We will continue to glean from her life. She genuinely cared deeply for us all. I miss her so much.

I continue to see her face and hear her voice. These are some of her favorite sayings:

"Mind yours P's and Q's"

"Think good thoughts"

"You were born an original don't die a copy"

"What's for you is for you"

"Never bring a C in the house; C's are average and unacceptable"

"Don't sweat the small stuff"

"God is great"

"Do your best"

"Make it happen"

"Don't take no mess"

"Become your best"

"Everybody is a somebody"

"If they knew better they would do better"

Mama will be forever loved, treasured and never forgotten. So glad God chose her for me. The best of the best. The purest form of love.

DR. YVONNE CAPEHART

WINNING WHILE WOUNDED

Obstacles, hardships, disappointments, and setbacks are at times unavoidable in life. It often happens in the most inopportune times and without notice. I too am a testament of how to overcome and survive adversity, after enduring various trials and tribulations in my life. Proverbs 18: 21 (KJV) says, "*Death and life are in the power of the tongue.*" While this is a widely quoted scripture used in today's churches; for me, growing up the power of the tongue has been a daunting echo of darkness in my life. As a young woman, in high school, my behavior, attention, and desires, did not reflect the promising future that I now have. I will admit, I made decision that gratified the moment before me, and not my destiny. A lack of focus and poor decision led me down a dark path filled with broken promises, dreams, and torn relationships.

Academically, I did not display strong academic excellence. I was visibly distracted by social interactions and the center of all the wrong attention. I became popular, and an eye catcher among the high school boys. During the last semester of my senior year, I began to seek guidance for my future endeavors (i.e. college, majors, careers, and etc.). Upon entering the school counselor's office, she smiled and showed an eagerness to initially help. She asked, "how may I help you?" A quick response, without processing my thoughts, I stated, "I am here for information on how to enroll into college." The counselor smiled, and began retrieving my academic records. A swift glance at my academic history and progress; her smiled quickly dwindled into a stare of dismay. She inhaled and exhaled with a brief moment of silence, she responded with words that would forever be etched in my heart. "Honey I am sorry, but you are not college material. Let's talk about a trade or something else." These words were not only statements of doubt, but a sound that would confirm what I had already thought and believed about myself.

I left thinking I was dumb and incapable of success. Yet, her words were no immediate shock, it only validated publicly what I had spoken privately to myself.

Rooted in a strong traditional family setting, filled with faith and prayer I had a grandmother who not only seen the potential in me, but knew the power of the decreed Word. My grandmother and I, Mother RB, my rock, was in church listening to a testimony shared by a lady who was healed from cancer, during that moment the sovereignty of God began to reign in my heart. On that same night, on the way home with my grandmother, I asked God to heal me from every word that wounded my heart, and heal me He did. I then made a conscience decision to turn my life around and become the woman I was designed to be and not the woman the world forced me to be.

Later, I enrolled into community college, and discontinued my studies after marriage. However, the passion to obtain my degree never left the sentiments of my heart. Determination arose in me, and I knew I was determined to make every word intended to wound me be the very words to create a win in me.

A few years later, I re-enrolled into college but not without professional guidance. Unfortunately, I had to seek educational counseling to address some underlying fears of entering college, which was nearly unbearable at times. The rejection from my youth, was getting the best of me, but somehow, I found the courage and perseverance to find myself at the brink of the admissions office. A perfect balance of fear and anticipation fluttered my heart. I was informed, my entrance exam scores where not high enough to secure admission.

I reserved the tears from falling as they welled in my eyes, instantly I felt the painful memory of the words and label of my high school counselor, "You are not college material," that began to flood my heart.

In the middle of disappointment, I was able to find a little ounce of courage, and I responded to the admission coordinator, "well, I can just take it again!" I knew that if I did not try again, those wounding words would win, instead me having the win over the wound. After three attempts of the entrance exam my scores where finally high enough to secure admission, but not without remedial courses.

During this academic progress, the Lord would order my steps and give me favor with instructors. Despite signs of academic struggles, they believed in me and were confident I would succeed. I was driven to achieve, I would receive tutoring early in the mornings and late at night.

Gradually, I went from denied entrance to full enrollment; from D's and F's to A's and B's; from remedial classes to core classes; and from high school diploma to degreed. This one win, would afford me the opportunity to create a series of academic wins in my life. I not only obtained my Associates Degree, but now I hold multiples degrees to include: a Bachelors in Education, a Master in Educational Leadership, and Doctrine in Counseling and Psychology.

Furthermore, I have authored eight books and have mentored women across the nation. I have spoken on multiple platforms, I am a business owner of various businesses, and above all, I have had a thriving and successful career for over twenty-five years.

After the completion of multiple degrees, I sought to find my retired high school guidance counselor only to thank her. As her wounding words have now been a pillar of immeasurable success and a driving force that has ignite perpetual wins on the inside of me. Also evoking purpose, perseverance, and ultimately pushed me to win under uncertainty.

CECILIA JAMES

YOUR LIFE CAN CHANGE IN THE BLINK OF AN EYE

Raised an only child by two incredible parents who were very hardworking but ultimately decided to get a divorce when I was seven had its challenges. The experience shaped and molded me into the resilient, emotionally tough woman I am today. I began working at an early age, went to college and got married at the age of 18. I married a wonderful man and we built a life together with our two amazing kids. I joined Mary Kay Cosmetics when I was just 21 years old. My husband owned his own business with his father and together we were working hard to build our future.

Although everything seemed amazing, we were not immune to life's challenges. The struggles of finances, our demanding schedules, family issues, as well as us just growing in different directions were prevalent for us. About 15 years into our marriage, my husband decided to sell his business because his father wanted to retire. He was not really sure what he wanted to do next, so we mutually agreed that he would stay home with our kids and I would build my Mary Kay business to the next level, but that brought many challenges on our marriage. He began to lose himself and could not seem to find his way and the financial pressure was heavy on me. I was exhausted from responsibility. Years of making things work, we realized we were really just two different people! We both did not know who we really were or, what we really wanted at 18 years old. Wanting two different things out of life now we ended up getting a divorce after 25 years of marriage. He is still an amazing person and is now happily remarried.

I have been grinding and growing for a quarter of a century and it might have seemed like I was a magnet to success, untouchable and unbreakable, but about five years ago everything changed. I lost my way. Have you ever heard the saying, "sometimes you win, sometimes you learn?" Well, I learned a bigger lesson than I ever thought I needed. We all make mistakes and if we learn from them, they will be stepping stones to living in our greatness. I lost sight and hope of so many things. I lost my passion. My affirmations went from, "I am the most emotionally healthy, mentally tough person I know" to looking in the mirror daily, my eyes full of tears saying, "stay strong, hold on. You can make it." I hope that by sharing this I give someone somewhere the strength to stand up for yourself or an awareness of a situation you may not have even realized or accepted you were in.

I met a man five years ago and I fell fast and hard. He seemed to do the same. Love was to the point of exhaustion. He sold me a dream and delivered a nightmare. It starts out as everything I ever wanted in a relationship. He was intriguing, generous, funny, spontaneous, confident, good looking, had a love for travel and people, the world, culture. I was having the time of my life and the life I never had. The last two years have been the most informative, happiest, hurtful, thoughtful, altering, molding, powerful accepting years of my life. The same person who said the sweetest things to me also said some of the meanest things I have ever heard in my life. And the same person who did some of the sweetest things, also did some of the meanest things.

He tried to install negative beliefs, chaos and dysfunction in my life. About 6 months into this relationship, a slow entry of deceit, lies, disrespect and cheating, he took everything I had and stomped on my soul until I was fully depleted. He was impossible to get along with, controlling, and in exchange expected perfectionism, respect, and all of my time and energy spent on him - robbing me of my most precious joys. Narcissist can do whatever they want, whenever they want but you are to remain loyal and perfect at all times. Always accusing me of the things he was guilty of.

A relationship is supposed to be a safe haven not a battlefield. Society might say I was weak, but the reality is I was someone with all the qualities a narcissistic sociopath wants, and I was the ultimate ego boost. If they can destroy you, they succeed in making you completely dependent on them. They are childlike, needy and malicious when they do not get their way. Isolation became privy and this unhealthy, abusive relationship was toxic. You would think someone like me would be smarter and know better than to fall for someone like this. I am strong, disciplined, independent, successful, dominant personality. Yet I was willing to exchange my independence and my identity for an illusion of a perfect future.

It took me a year to realize what a toxic situation I was in and that I was slowly being destroyed. That it was not really love but control and narcissistic supply. You do not destroy people that you love. I often say that people's personalities should fascinate you and not frustrate you. I was fascinated in the beginning. I was being wowed. I was the perfect prey. Positive, deeply empathetic, focused on others, a people pleaser, slow to judge, tolerant, an eye for finding the good in others, and a high tolerance for emotional pain.

I lost my mind trying to understand who he was. I traded my self-respect for his attention. Narcissists can only maintain normalcy for short spurts of time. Gas lighting, Love bombing. Me trying to hang on to all my healthy success habits that he gradually and very discreetly took away from me.

Many people stood by me while others did not understand. Some judged me and others lent me a shoulder to cry on.

What a narcissist lacks is their own self-control because they have none; they try to control you. What they despise is your strength. These people are like parasites that attach themselves to kind and generous people and they contaminate your thoughts and moods. Five years ago, I was sharing my survival story from parasite in my body that almost cost me my life and now I am sharing this survival story of human parasite that tried to take over my life as well. These parasites are skilled manipulators, pathological liars, emotionally unstable.

I owe myself a big apology for putting up with all of it for as long as I did. I guess I thought it would change. I thought I could fix him. I was letting him destroy me while I was trying to save him, but sometimes your heart needs more time to accept what your mind already knows.

I know could not have survived this without everything I learned in Mary Kay. Whatever your battle is, start dealing with it! Cancel that pity party! Go get the support you need. Take ownership of getting to know and fall in love with your true self. Be driven enough to find the life you want and courageous enough to chase it. If you are dealing with verbal or physical abuse or any other forms of abuse, just know that you can start over and start to love yourself the way you were always meant to be loved. You do not have to wait on anyone else to do it for you.

Mary Kay Ash used to say, "if, just one more woman discovers how great she is it will be a great day." I hope you know you have the power from within to rise up and take control of your life and that you always fight for whatever you feel that you deserve.

I am still healing and, one day, I will be stronger because of all of this. I will be wiser than ever. I know now that you cannot heal in the same environment where you got sick. I still feel the grief of it all on some days, some days the pain is still unimaginable, but I know that this story is not a story about my flaws, weaknesses or mistakes. It is ok that I believe in people. It is ok that I trust people to be as good as I am. I trust people to love as I do and so it is truly a testament of all of my best qualities. Shame is not my burden to carry. Neither is blame. The bible tells us in James 1:1 that we develop trials and temptations to make us stronger, whole, more mature and complete, not lacking anything.

One day I woke up and decided I did not want to feel like this anymore and so I pulled the plug. I was exhausted emotionally, physically and spiritually. I felt like I was a hundred years old. I looked like it too and just like that, I decided that my peace was my priority and that if it cost me my peace, the price was too high!

CRISETTE ELLIS

YOUR FAITH MUST PREVAIL!

Charles Dickens wrote a novel in 1859 entitled *A Tale Of Two Cities*. The setting is in London and Paris and gives a historical view of before and after the French Revolution. Dickens opens his book by saying, "It was the best of times and the worst of times." It is a historical novel that captures what was going on in Europe, but for me it was more personal. I have experienced what this statement means first hand.

One might ask, how is it possible to experience both the best and the worst times of your life at the very same time? Trust me when I tell you, it is possible! For me, this statement became a reality when my third child Kiersten Marie Ellis was born. I had already given birth to two healthy children, Kiera and Charles within the past 3 years. Kiera was just two years old and Charles IV (Buddy) was only 4 months when I found out that I was pregnant again with my third child. I was completely shocked! It happened so soon after having my second child, Charles, that I was still on maternity leave. I was stressed out about telling my manager that not only was I pregnant again but that I could not come back to work as planned because of some complications I was having and my gynecologist advised against it. I eventually got up the nerve to tell my manager. I began to mentally prepare myself for what it would be like to have a newborn baby, a 1-year-old and a 3-year-old toddler all at the same time!

Let me digress for a minute. You have heard the saying be careful what you wish for you just might get it? I can remember after graduating from Michigan State University, all I could think and pray about was getting hired by a Fortune 500 company. I just knew that if I was to get hired by a Fortune 500 company, I was destined to be a corporate executive. You can imagine the excitement I felt when I was hired by Ford Motor Company as a Program Control Analyst right after graduation! I just knew I was on my way to the top. My life was headed in the right direction and I was about to start living the life of my dreams. I knew that if I worked hard and gave Ford my best, I would eventually move up the corporate ladder.

Well, that all started to change after I got married and became pregnant with my first child Kiera 2 years later. After giving birth to my baby girl, something inside of me suddenly changed. It was if a monkey wrench had been thrown into my "dreams" and now all of a sudden all I could think about was wanting to be at home with my baby. Moving up the corporate ladder was no longer important to me. I remember thinking, "maybe this feeling will go away and my desire to chase my dream of being a corporate executive will come back." I had no idea that it was possible to stay at home with my baby and still be the executive women that I envisioned for myself. I did not know that I could have my cake and eat it too, but I would soon find out!

While at home on maternity leave, a friend of mine by the name of Virginia Warfield introduced me to the Mary Kay opportunity. She knew I was at home on maternity leave and that I was looking for something to do part-time. Everything that was shared with me about the Mary Kay opportunity excited me. I loved the company's philosophy, God first, family second and career third, as well as the fact that Mary Kay offered me the flexibility to make a schedule where I could work the business around my family as opposed working my family around my corporate job. At 6 months pregnant, I decided to become an Independent Beauty Consultant with Mary Kay and quickly found myself moving up the Mary Kay career ladder. Everything was perfect! I was really living my dream. I was on target to earn my first Mary Kay career car, but soon after that I went into labor two weeks before my due date. My husband Charles was out of town on a ministry assignment, so my sister Karen and her husband Darryl came to my house and rushed me to the hospital. My daughter Kiersten was born by cesarean section and, little did I know, her birth would change my life forever. For the first time, I would truly understand the meaning of those words by Charles Dickens, because it was literally both the best and worst times of my life.

I will never forget, after I delivered Kiersten, I saw her for only a brief moment when the doctor quickly took her away. I waited for what seemed to be the longest hour of my life for the doctor to come into my room with the most horrific news for any mother to hear. I was informed that my daughter had been diagnosed with a genetic skin disease called Epidermolysis Bullosa EB for short. Epidermolysis Bullosa is an extremely rare disease and the odds of having a child born with EB with no prior family history was something like one-in-a-million.

He said it was a rare disease, best described as a genetic condition that causes the skin to be very fragile and to blister easily with even the slightest bit of friction. Layers of skin would eventually move and separate causing open wounds and extreme pain.

What a surreal moment this was for me. How could I have possibly delivered two very healthy babies less than 3 years before Kiersten and now here I am with a child with such a serious disease? No one in our family had ever heard of this disease and were unaware of any such genetic disorders. I just could not understand how God could allow this to happen to our daughter. I could feel despair, fear and helplessness begin to take over. I told myself over and over again to stay positive and trust God in an attempt to calm my fears and keep a positive mentality. I said, "Chuck and I will just have to deal with it, have faith and pray for God to heal her." After explaining to us the seriousness of the disease, the doctor began to tell me that the chances of my daughter living longer than six months were highly unlikely and instantly, my faith was shattered, my fears ignited and the floodgates of my eyes opened up for the tears to flow. The doctor left me in the room by myself with my thoughts to come to grips with what he had just told me, and the pity party began. Now that it was just me and God in my hospital room, I began to cry out to God and ask him why? Why me? Why our baby? What had I ever done to deserve this? You see, in my mind I had been a good and faithful servant to God and to my family and I had to tell God that I did not deserve this from him. I wanted to make Him feel bad about letting this happen to my baby and to our family.

I thought my life was going in the right direction. I was living my best life! I was married to the love of my life, had two beautiful, healthy children about to have my third, and my Mary Kay business was going great. I would have never envisioned something like this happening to me and yet here I was. In the silence I could hear the Lord speaking. He was saying to me, "who are you? Why should some rain not fall in your life? What makes you any different from the rest of my children who suffer?" He had taken me back to the day 3 years ago when I gave birth to my healthy daughter Kiera, then he took me back to the day he blessed me with a healthy baby boy "Buddy" and reminded me that blessings have been flowing steady in my life and that I should remain grateful for them and not dwell on the misfortune,. Yet, it is only human nature to focus more on our crisis and less on our blessings. God had to remind me that in spite of what I was going through at that moment I still had a lot to be thankful for.

On May 25th, 1994, Kiersten Marie Ellis went home to be with the Lord and although my family and I were praying for a different outcome, God had spoken. Through the pain and the tears, my faith in God and his ultimate purpose for my family and my life was evident - that I was to tell my testimony and let it encourage someone who may be going though a similar situation to show them that when you find yourself in a crisis right in the midst of your blessed life to keep celebrating your blessed life. Never forget not even for a second just how blessed you truly are.

Yes, bad things happen and can happen at the most inconvenient times, but through your faith and belief in God, you will be rewarded with God's grace and his mercy. My husband and I prayed together and had so many other people praying on our behalf and on behalf of our daughter. Yes, we had days when we were encouraged as well as days when we were overwhelmed and feeling defeated and sometimes our faith wavered, but it was imperative to keep going and to never give up and remember that God would give me strength, comfort, and peace, and reward me for every tear I cried. I realize now that just as we should trust and praise God when things are going fine that it is equally just as important to trust Him when life is hard and gives you challenges, because guess what, the trials and challenges are blessings too! They are opportunities to grow in our relationship with God. To learn valuable life lessons. That is just what I did. I grew closer to God and got to know Him deeper and more intimately, because I had to learn how to trust and depend on Him more than I ever had before. I needed to experience the God that promised He would never leave or forsaken me! God truly showed me through answered prayers that I was not alone.

I believe that every Christian will experience a time in their life when their faith is challenged, and they have no choice but to trust and believe in God. It is only in these times that we truly get to experience God on a higher level first hand. Psalms 119:71 says, *"It is good for me that I have been afflicted; that I might learn thy statutes."*

I can testify that it does not feel good and you will not always understand, but that is why we walk by faith and not by sight. If you focus on your situation more than the lessons and the blessings you will only fall into depression and fear the unknown. You have to stay prayed up and completely sold out to the purpose that God has for your life, even through the pain and tears that may come along the way.

Jeremiah 29:11 says, *"For I know the thoughts I think toward you says the Lord, they are thoughts of peace and not of evil to give you an expected end."* You can take comfort in knowing that whatever test and trials that come your way, God is on your side and giving you ultimate favor. Job said, *"Though He slay me yet will I trust Him,"* and to that I say amen.

My friends, take courage in these words that I found in Romans 8:28, it says *"And we know that all things work together for the good of those who love God, to those who are called according to his purpose."* Live in the truth and the light of God's promises and I promise you will always prevail.

SCRIPTURES TO INSPIRE YOU TO
STAND ON YOUR GREATNESS!

CHAPTER 16

WHY ARE YOU SITTING ON YOUR GREATNESS?

WORDS TO ENCOURAGE YOU ON YOUR JOURNEY. REPEAT THEM EVERY MORNING!

Philippians 4:6-7
I will not be anxious about anything instead in everything through prayer and petition with thanksgiving, I will tell my request to God.
In the Name and Through The Power Of Jesus Christ!

John 16:23-24
My Father will give me whatever I ask in His name. I will ask and I will receive, and my joy will be completed.
In The Name And Through The Power Of Jesus Christ!

Proverbs 10:22
The blessings of the Lord makes me rich, and He adds no sorrow with it.
In The Name And Through The Power Of Jesus Christ

Psalm 32:8
The Lord will instruct me and teach me in the way I should go. He will council and watch over me He will guide me with His eyes.
In The Name And Through The Power Of Jesus Christ!

Jeremiah 31:3
In a far, off Land the Lord will manifest Himself to me. He will say to me _____ (put you name here) I have loved you with everlasting love, that is why I continue to be faithful to you.
In The Name And Through The Power Of Jesus Christ!

Ephesians 6:16
I will take up the shield of faith with which I can extinguish all the flaming arrows of the enemy!
In The Name And Through The Power Of Jesus Christ!

Mathew 6:33
I will seek first the kingdom of God and His righteousness. When I do that all things shall be added to me.
In The Name And Through The Power Of Jesus Christ!

Proverbs 3:5-6
I will trust in the Lord with all my heart and lean not on my own understanding; I will acknowledge you, in all your ways for it is You that will make my paths straight.
In The Name And Through The Power Of Jesus Christ!

Psalm 139:14
I praise You because I am fearfully and wonderfully made; by you, your works are wonderful, and I know them full well.
In The Name And Through The Power Of, Jesus Christ!

Romans12:2
I will not be conformed to the patterns of this world, but I will be transformed by the renewal of my mind. Then I will know God's good and pleasing and perfect will for my life.
In The Name and Through The Power Of Jesus Christ!

Psalm 37:7
I wait patiently on the Lord. I wait confidently for Him.
In The Name And Through The Power Of Jesus Christ!

Psalm 21:6
For You grant me lasting blessings you gave me great joy by allowing me into your presence!
In The Name And Through The Power Of Jesus Christ!

Hebrew 4:16
Therefore; I will confidently approach the throne of favor, to receive mercy and favor whenever I need help.
In The Name And Through The Power Of Jesus Christ!

QUOTES TO INSPIRE YOU TO
STAND ON YOUR GREATNESS!

CHAPTER 17

WHY ARE YOU SITTING ON YOUR GREATNESS?

GREAT QUOTES FROM POWERFUL PEOPLE!

"Think Like a queen. A queen is not afraid to fail. Failure is another steppingstone to greatness." Oprah Winfrey

"You were designed for accomplishment, engineered for success, and endowed with the seeds of greatness." Zig Ziglar

"Never underestimate the power of dreams and the influence of the human spirit. We are all the same in this notion: the potential for greatness lives within each of us." Wilma Rudolph

"Greatness is not measured by what a woman accomplishes, but by the opposition she has overcome to reach her goal." Dorothy Height

"You are destined for greatness believe in yourself and go for it. Greatness comes by surrounding yourself with great people." Alahdal A. Hussein

"Be not afraid of greatness some are born great, some achieve greatness, and others have greatness thrust upon them." William Shakespeare

"Great things in business are never done by one person. They're done by a team of people." Steve Jobs

"Greatness is inside all of us but first we must choose to be great."
Nora Shariff Borden

"Greatness come from the desire to do extraordinary things."
Nora Shariff Borden

"Don't limit yourself. Many people limit themselves to what they think they can do. Your can as far your mind lets you. What you believe, remember you can achieve." Mary Kay Ash

"Great thoughts speak only to the thoughtful mind, bur great actions speak to all mankind." Theodore Roosevelt

"If we cannot see the possibility of greatness, how can we dream it?" Lee Strasberg

"Keep away from people who try to belittle your ambitions. Small people always do that, but the really great make you feel that you, too, can become great." Mark Twain

"A woman's greatness is all she needs to hold on to when opposition show up." Nora Shariff Borden

'When you speak greatness into the lives of others greatness will come back to you." Nora Shariff Borden."

"Great things happen when people have Great expectations." Nora Shariff Borden

"Great things happen when you believe they can." Nora Shariff Borden

"No matter who you are, greatness awaits you all you have do is believe and walk in it." Nora Shariff Borden

"If you're walking down the right path and you're willing to keep walking, eventually you'll make progress." President, Barack Obama

"Whatever is bringing you down, get rid of it. Because you'll find that when you're free your true self comes out." Tina Turner

"Every great dream begins with a dreamer. Always remember, you have within you the strength, the patience, and the passion to reach for the stars to change the world." Harriet Tubman

"Greatness occurs when your children love you, when your critics respect you and when you have peace of mind." Quincy Jones

"A made up mind can do anything all you have to do is decide what you want."
Nora Shariff Borden

"Always stay true to yourself and never let what somebody else says distract you from your goals." Michelle Obama

"Always be careful of your circle of influence. The right circle can lift you up and the wrong circle can weigh you down!" Nora Shariff Borden

"If you don't like something, change it. If you can't change it, change your attitude." Maya Angelou

"I have come to believe over and over again that what is most important to me must be spoken, made verbal and shared, even at the risk of having it bruised or misunderstood." Audre Lorde

"No one should negotiate their dreams. Dreams must be free to flee and fly high. You should never surrender your dreams." Jesse Jackson

"Just don't give up what you're trying to do. Where there is love and inspiration, I don't think you can go wrong." Ella Fitzgerald

"It's not the load that breaks you down, It's the way you carry it." Lena Horne

"Have a Vision. Be demanding." Colin Powell

"You're obligated to win. You're obligated to keep trying to do the best you can every day." Marian Wright Edelman

"I have learned over the years that when one's mind is made up, this diminishes fear; knowing what must be done does away with fear." Rosa Parks

"Sometimes, what you're looking for is already there." Aretha Franklin

"When you are seeking to bring big plans to fruition it is important with whom you regularly associate with." Mark Twain

Please contact me at info@bwotmfg.com for speaking engagements.

For more information about business women on the move for God visit us at www.bwotmf.com

Other books available by Nora Shariff Borden include:

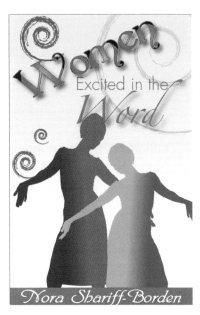